7/19/18

Challenge

Confront

CHANGE!

the table activities. When I surveyed participants after the session, 72 percent indicated that they would Strongly Agree or Agree that as a result of the StrengthsFinder workshop, they came away with greater knowledge about their personal talents. Thank you, Chad, for the time and energy you put into our workshop."

— Kristy Davis, Associate Director, Academic Support Resources, University of Minnesota

"Chad's story and efforts to prevent hazing in college fraternity settings is a powerful example of how to turn one's pain into power. Chad's speaking and coaching style reveals an understanding of, and commitment to, building up people and communities in a way that could only be accomplished by someone who has borne witness to the suffering that can be caused by The Bystander Effect."

— Shawn Furey, Drug and Alcohol Counselor, Blue Sky Counseling

"Chad was such an amazing speaker to start off the Sisters for Success women empowerment program. He showed that this was an issue that both genders need to work on. He empowered the women to start their story through real life and pop culture examples. He comes prepared and is extremely flexible. I enjoyed very much working with him."

— Chloe Edwards, Project and Digital Marketing Specialist, JackRabbit

"Imagine reading a book that takes you from feeling stuck in a rut to lots of light bulb moments to inspire, motivate, and drive you full force to pursue your dreams. Here is the gamechanger. Now read it; then put the simple, easy, and powerful steps into action to jumpstart your life and focus on what really matters."

— Susan Friedmann, CSP, International Bestselling Author of *Riches in Niches: How to Make It BIG in a small Market*

"I heard Chad speak at the Fall 2013 Minnesota College Personnel Association (MCPA) conference on the topic of 'The hero's journey.' I immediately asked him if he could tailor the presentation for a training for my Section Leaders (student mentors) who facilitate the First Year Experience course in the University of Minnesota's College of Liberal Arts. Chad's training session exceeded all expectations! He kept a room of sixty upper-class undergraduate students actively engaged, several approached him after the training session to continue the conversation, and many have passed on the knowledge to the first-year students they are mentoring! Kudos to Chad for being so adaptable and approachable. This is information that can be tailored to any setting and any audience! Thank you, Chad!"

— Jennifer Endres, Program Director, Office for Student Experience in the College of Liberal Arts, University of Minnesota

"I had the fortunate opportunity to meet with Chad in two sittings, with my coworkers and individually. I am surprised the university does not have more promotion around him and the benefits of StrengthsFinder. Chad helped our team understand ourselves and each other through our strengths and how we could optimize our communication and productivity. Individually, he opened my eyes to the benefits of knowing and owning my strengths not just for the workplace but for all interactions in my life."

— Michaela Dean, Operations and Communications Manager, Gary S. Holmes Center for Entrepreneurship, Carlson School of Management, University of Minnesota

"In *Building Up Without Tearing Down*, Chad Ellsworth tells us some hard-hitting truths about how we initiate people into our organizations. Then he reveals how we can change this process so everyone comes out ahead. It's a hero's journey worth taking."

— Nicole Gabriel, Author of *Finding Your Inner Truth* and *Stepping Into Your Becoming*

"I had the privilege of co-instructing a class with Chad. He is a diligent and dedicated educator who skillfully inspires students to realize and maximize their own leadership potential. He authentically leads by his character-filled example and motivates his students to learn and achieve with creative and thought-provoking lesson plans, classroom content, and group work."

— Maggie Harris, Faculty Teaching Specialist and
Level Coordinator, University of Minnesota

"I became acquainted with Chad through LeaderShape. A graduate of our Institute program and member of our community, Chad presented a webinar to the LeaderShape community last year. He guided the participants through a reflection of their own leadership journey and did so through a vehicle that we can all understand—the journey of a hero! His commitment to the development of leadership in others and his willingness to invest in their growth is obvious."

— Kristen Bendon Hyman, Vice President, LeaderShape, Inc.

"Chad provided me with invaluable insight into my strengths as a Business Analyst. By listening constructively to my thoughts about the StrengthsFinder results I received, he was able to identify how I could better leverage my skill-set, and help me in moving closer to my professional development goals."

— Chris Johnson, Business Analyst, Academic Support Resources,
University of Minnesota

"I had the pleasure to work with Chad on multiple projects and have always been impressed by his capabilities and knowledge base. He brings a level of professionalism and enthusiasm that inspires those around him and raises the bar for his colleagues and coworkers. Chad is a wonderful resource, mentor, and friend. He provides guidance to hundreds of students who look up to him as a leader in student development."

— Ed Kim, Assistant Director of Campus Life, University of St. Thomas

"Chad is leading the line in using heroism and the hero's journey in combatting the negative aspects of the college system. His approach comes from direct experience and a long stint in the field, making it hard to beat. This book will be a great tool for anyone wanting to create cultural change."

— Matt Langdon, Founder, The Hero Round Table

"There is a hero inside all of us. All of us can hear it calling out, ready to emerge. But are we willing to let that hero out? Chad Ellsworth delivers a powerful guide to empowering and emboldening all of us to live as the kind of people—the heroes—that we are all born to be."

— Matthew Mattson, Speaker and Author of
Social Excellence: We Dare You

"Chad has long been an inspiration to me for his research and work on behalf of hazing prevention. I was grateful when he agreed to volunteer for HazingPrevention.Org, then serve on the board and then become its chair. This book is just the latest in a long string of incredible contributions to this important work, but it is without a doubt his best. The excellent writing, personal stories, and solid recommendations offered provide great guidance for any student who wants to belong without being belittled or abused."

— Tracy Maxwell, Founder, HazingPrevention.Org and
Author of *Being Single, With Cancer: A Solo Survivor's
Guide to Life, Love, Health and Happiness*

"Who doesn't want to be a hero? In *Building Up Without Tearing Down*, Chad Ellsworth provides us with the Heroic Arts we can all apply to our own lives. This book will be invaluable for teachers, managers, business owners, coaches, and anyone who wants to help others achieve their full potential."

— Tyler R. Tichelaar, PhD and Award-Winning Author
of *Narrow Lives* and *The Best Place*

"We brought Chad to RIT to be our 2017 Hazing Prevention Week Keynote Speaker and we could not have been happier with our choice. Chad was able to share his deeply compelling story with our fraternity and sorority community, which had a significant impact on the members in attendance and became a call to action to prevent stories like his from being replicated at RIT. Chad's story and presentation style were very engaging and showed the effects of hazing, but he also gave instruction on how to prevent it from happening again. Chad's story should be heard by everyone to show the dangers of hazing."

— Eric Pope, Associate Director for Fraternity and Sorority Life and Assessment, Rochester Institute of Technology

"Chad has helped Phi Gamma Delta out in several capacities. His two presentations at Fiji Academy, 'Let's Talk About Hazing' and 'Power on Your Chapter, Power on Yourself,' have been rated very highly by our undergraduate and graduate members. Members have gone as far as saying, 'Highlight of my Academy.' Chad also helps the fraternity out with curriculum writing. He is a great sounding board for curriculum ideas and thinks outside the box when it comes to experiential learning opportunities."

— Todd Rotgers, Senior Director of Undergraduate Services, Phi Gamma Delta

"Chad and I got connected through a series of mutual connections when I was looking for a career coach. I have had many career changes and was looking for help defining what a good career theme for me was that I could work toward. Chad was so helpful in asking the right questions and defining activities for me that brought up common themes across my career and beyond that helped pinpoint what a good fit for me would be. He really helped bring to the surface all those important things that I had a hard time seeing. I am so grateful for his guidance and insight."

— Mirna Vela, English Teacher at Berlitz Corporation

"Chad is a powerful, moving, and truly inspirational speaker. He encourages heroism and uses his experiences to help others. I'm excited for his upcoming book and for all the wisdom he has to share."

— Dr. Janina Scarlet, Speaker and Author of *Superhero Therapy: A Hero's Journey through Acceptance and Commitment Therapy*

"No one should have to be bullied in their school or workplace. Instead, we all have the potential to be heroes and inspire others to be the same. In *Building Up Without Tearing Down*, Chad Ellsworth offers us tools for how we can all create our own destinies within our organizations and personal lives and create win-win situations for everyone."

— Patrick Snow, Publishing Coach and International Best-Selling Author of *Creating Your Own Destiny* and *Boy Entrepreneur*

"As the former president of the board for HazingPrevention.Org, I was not only comfortable, but honored to hand over the leadership to Chad. He is a strong and visionary, yet caring, leader for this organization. His vision has led this non-profit to become a recognized leader in preventing and eradicating hazing at all levels."

— Allison Swick-Duttine, Director of Fraternity/ Sorority Life, SUNY Plattsburgh

"I have known Chad for a couple of years and have always admired his knowledge and skills related to StrengthsFinder. When he became a Gallup-Certified Strengths Coach, I knew I had to learn more. He coached my husband and me in a conversation around our strengths and gave us great tools to continue the conversation. Chad is an impeccable connector and communicator. When Chad speaks, we should all listen to what he has to say."

— Kari Wilson, Program Coordinator, Undergraduate Business Career Center, Carlson School of Management, University of Minnesota

THERE IS A HERO IN ALL OF US

BUILDING UP
WITHOUT TEARING DOWN

HOW TO CULTIVATE HEROIC LEADERSHIP IN YOU AND YOUR ORGANIZATION

CHAD ELLSWORTH

AVIVA
PUBLISHING
New York

BUILDING UP WITHOUT TEARING DOWN
How to Cultivate Heroic Leadership in You and Your Organization

Published by:
Aviva Publishing
Lake Placid, NY
(518) 523-1320
www.AvivaPubs.com

Chad Ellsworth
Telephone: 651-233-3533
Email: Chad@CapedCoaching.com
www.BuildingUpWithoutTearingDown.com
www.CapedCoaching.com

ISBN: 978-1-947937-29-1

Library of Congress Control Number: 2018904251

Editor: Tyler Tichelaar
Cover Designer: Nicole Gabriel / Angel Dog Productions
Interior Book Layout: Nicole Gabriel / Angel Dog Productions
Author Photo: Erik Smith / HSP Imaging Inc.

Every attempt has been made to source properly all quotes.

Printed in the United States of America

First Edition

ACKNOWLEDGMENTS

I have been fortunate to have so many compassionate, encouraging, and insightful people throughout my life, and I thank them as my own personal team of heroes for their contributions to who I am:

Goldie & William Aden, Scott Allison, Travis Apgar, Ashley Artrip, Jennifer Baddin, Denise W. Barreto, Laura Bloomberg, James Buboltz, Dan Bureau, Brett Culp, "Super Ewan" Drum, Gary Dunham, Chloe Edwards, Keith Edwards, Steve Ehrfurth, Darin Eich, Zeno Franco, Shawn Furey, Adam Goldstein, Bill Grohs, Maggie Harris, Karen Kurotsuchi Inkelas, Ellie Jacques, Anna Jankord, Susan Komives, Matt Langdon, Kyle Lau, Susan LeBlanc, Matt Levine, Chris Lowney, Dustin Manhart, Joel Mattek, Tom Matson, Matt Mattson, Tracy Maxwell, Marylu McEwen, Erika Michalski, Ali Miller, Lisa Novack, Kim Novak, Hank Nuwer, Akila Pai, Norm Pollard, Eric Pope, Sasanehsaeh Pyawasay, David Rendall, Robert Riggs, Todd Rotgers, Janina Scarlet, Katie Selby, Nikki Letawsky Shultz, Patrick Takaya Solomon, Kathy Stern, Matt Supple, Elizabeth Svoboda, Kai Takatsuka, Charles Van Rossum, Carol Warren, Megan Gaffney Wells, Dave Westol, Amelious Whyte, Jessica Gendron Williams, Matthew Winkler, Richard Wood, Dan Wrona, and John Zacker.

I could not have completed this massive project without the expertise and insight of Patrick Snow, Tyler Tichelaar, and Nicole Gabriel, who guided me through the process of writing, editing, and designing this book.

I have been blessed with a helpful and loving family, including William and Valerie Ellsworth, Troy Ellsworth, Joe and Cheryl Flaherty, and Kelly Flaherty.

In addition to my family by birth, Paul DeBettignies, Ryan Holmes, Trevor Johnson, Ed Kim, Joe Kopp, Sean Morrison, Mike Murphy, and Chris Wegener are among the brothers whom I have chosen rather than received by birth, and I am thankful for everything they have given me. Without Chris, Joe, and Trevor's actions one night, I would not have found the path that led to this book.

Finally, I am deeply indebted to my wife, Kristin, for her belief in me, her encouragement, and her patience as I pursued my goal of publishing this book. I am also indebted to my sons, Joey and Paul, who not only gave up some of their time with "Daddy," but also have inspired me from the very beginning of their lives to be the best father and man I can be.

Thank you all.

CONTENTS

FOREWORD

Chad Ellsworth always promised me that one day he would write a book. Now he has done so, and it is a valuable addition to the sparse literature devoted to hazing as well as the importance of positive rather than negative reinforcement of values in any organization. Chad writes with a valuable perspective seldom seen in a hazing and leadership expert. He himself was brutally hazed as a student, so he knows firsthand how he and hundreds of thousands of other fraternity members were seduced into abusive initiation rites in order to gain membership into a high-status fraternal organization.

Thus, Chad's book manages to convey the personal horror of a young man trapped behind fraternity-closed doors individually and in the company of his fellow pledges to endure actions ranging from sadistic to borderline criminal—actions that no one in any organization should have to endure.

Building Up Without Tearing Down nimbly crosses from narrative storytelling to the latest research from scholarly authors and leading behavioral gurus. Always, the book keeps a consistent message. Fraternal groups and all organizations have value and even values, but a good percentage of them perversely create trust by exerting a high cost in ordeals as a way of imposing trust and solidarity. As Chad writes, onboarding new members of an organization is a transformative experience, and those driving these processes can demand their new members undergo rituals involving alcohol, degradation, and humiliation. The situations may differ in organizations, but the results are the same when organizations seek to tear down members to reshape them into what they want. The result is that the "changed" new members are not always better people, nor are their organizations necessarily better than those that offer a positive newcomer educational training experience. Chad urges a challenging onboarding process for all organizations in which an initiate, new member, or new employee learns the value of unselfishness and the quest for greater purpose that the best organizations cherish.

Chad's emphasis is always on a positive, even heroic, journey for new members. He stresses both the importance of mentoring and the need for each individual's "unique journey" into adulthood, responsibility, and success. "We resolve to create meaningful, positive, and yet challenging, rites of passage," he writes. "We have the power and the responsibility to instill the courage, skills, and strength that not only protect our members and organizations, but also power the future of our communities and organizations in increasingly fragmented and turbulent times."

The heart and soul of Chad's mission and message is this: "To find success in this fight for the soul of our organizations, we not only need environmental, social, and systemic solutions, but also courageous individuals and groups with the conviction, integrity, and will to lead the way."

Building Up Without Tearing Down appears at a turbulent time when it is most needed. *The New York Times* and *Boston Globe* have both championed articles demanding an end to Greek life in the wake of four young men dying while pledging in 2017. Hazing, coupled with unbridled alcohol/illegal drug consumption and an alarming number of sexual assaults at fraternity houses, has brought out the voices of victims and their families to demand wholesale changes. School administrators such as Pennsylvania State University President Eric J. Barron have insisted in media interviews that shutting down the Greek system is an option now on the table. In addition, countless studies show that most employees hate their jobs and feel unfulfilled in them. This situation is the result of organizations failing to share their values and purposes with their people to make them feel like an integral and productive part of the organization. Whether a business, fraternity, or nonprofit, organizations everywhere need to instill values in their members that build up rather than tear down.

As the author of five books on hazing, including the 2018 *Hazing: Destroying Young Lives*, I have had the privilege of interacting with many hazing activists and reformers over my forty years with hazing education as my academic specialty. Chad has always impressed me with his own scholarly research, his work as a former president of HazingPrevention. Org, and his devotion to family. At a memorable national conference put on by HPO in Maine some years ago, he asserted himself as a genuine leading authority in the push for antihazing measures.

Clearly, Chad has taken his own quest for a heroic identity for his fraternity and himself and developed a path and principles others can follow to choose the heroic, hazing-free path. Thus, Chad's book is a narrative, a text, and a workbook teaching individuals and groups how to protect and empower new members.

As a fraternity member, Chad saw the consequences of pledging a troubled chapter that had to be disciplined by the school and national organization. Later, his quest for a positive fraternal experience led him to a second chapter, an alliance with Theta Chi, whose members rescued him from the troubled organization in a dramatic way, and his lifelong conviction that Robert Frost's famous road-less-traveled was and is the "hero-path."

In 2000, Chad confessed to me that he had found that he possessed the capacity to become a leader. With this new book, I can say with assurance, that Chad has also now found his voice.

I wish all of Chad's readers a good, safe journey as individuals and group members in the Hero's Journey espoused by Joseph Campbell.

Hank Nuwer

Author of *Broken Pledges*, *The Hazing Reader*, *High School Hazing*, *Wrongs of Passage*, and *Hazing: Destroying Young Lives*

Franklin, Indiana and Warsaw, Poland

Introduction

FINDING THE HERO INSIDE OF YOU

"Promise me you'll always remember: You're braver than you believe, and stronger than you seem, and smarter than you think."

— A. A. Milne

As clear as can be, you see your goal right there in front of you.

Imagine yourself reaching out, straining and stretching every fiber of muscle in your body, extending your arm as far as you can toward your goal. You can feel your fingers just inches away from grasping that which you want.

In that moment, you realize that something is holding you back. No, *someone* is holding you back. You can feel his/her hand with a strong hold on your forearm. The more you reach, the more he/she resists, matching your strength.

Just then, you turn to look behind you and what you see stops you in your tracks.

Although the person you see holding you back is unmistakable, you refuse to believe your eyes.

How could this person do this to you? *Why* would he or she do this to you? It doesn't make any sense!

Now realizing the identity of this person, you turn to break free, knowing that he or she can match you in strength and will.

When you read this, you may have had an immediate reaction, imagining a specific person or a group of people. Who came to mind first for you?

Would you be surprised if the one person most likely to hold you back were you?

You are your own greatest inhibitor.

Do you find yourself frustrated with the current state of your life? Or maybe a specific part of your life? At the end of the day, maybe you don't know whether "this" is what you want to do with your life. Maybe you look at what's going on in your organization, your community, or the world, and you think you could be doing more to make a difference. No, you know you *should* do more.

Or maybe you look at your group, your organization, or your team, and you see some things going wrong. They may or may not be illegal and may not even violate any policies, but they definitely are not the right way to do things. We do not join organizations to stagnate or to become lesser versions of ourselves. We join them to develop our potential.

So, why doesn't somebody do something?

You're somebody, aren't you?

But maybe you're afraid. Maybe you think you're the only one who thinks that way. Or maybe you look at yourself and think you're not the kind of person who does something like that. You may think you lack some sort of authority or position of power. You wonder, or even worry, what your family, friends, classmates, neighbors, and even complete strangers will think of you.

Despite all of that, there is a nagging feeling inside of you. It feels like there is *something* you cannot not do.

How do I know? I've been there, too. In fact, even now, I find myself there.

The difference between when I had that nagging feeling in the past and when I have it now is that I no longer get stuck in that feeling. I know how to move forward. More than that, I know how to move others forward.

In this book, you will learn not only the skills and strategies for becoming the best version of yourself, but once you have gone down that path, you'll learn how you can guide others down it as well.

The ancient Greek philosophers believed the highest goal for one's life was to achieve a concept they called "eudaimonia," which can be translated as a combination of "well-being" and "well-doing." It may be best captured by one of Aristotle's most famous quotes, "Where your talents and the needs of the world cross lies your calling."

If you read this book and stop there, absolutely nothing in your life will change, except you will have a little less time. However, if you read this book and implement the strategies and tools herein, you will find the hero inside you and develop the tactics for cultivating heroic leadership in your organization. For this reason, this book not only shows you the path and provides both well-known and lesser-known examples of people throughout time who have traveled that path, but it also challenges you to reflect on your own life and find opportunities for implementing each chapter's main principles through reflective exercises.

In many ways, this book is a manifestation of my own twenty-plus-year journey toward leadership, which began when I experienced hazing as a first-year college student. At the time, we were told we would be "torn down" so we could be "built back up," a promise that was left wholly unfulfilled. However, it was through that experience that I began searching for, studying, and implementing strategies in which we can empower people to become the best versions of themselves. As

I pursued my master's degree, studying counseling and leadership, I conducted a major research study on hazing across different types of organizations, which led me to publish several articles based on my findings.

For this reason, this book begins with "Emerging from Hazing" in Part I, because my experience with and understanding of hazing has been foundational to this work. In short, I could not tell this story without starting there. As a direct result of my own dramatic experience with hazing, I knew that destructive and dysfunctional organizations were doing irreparable harm to individuals and communities, and themselves, as well.

Organizations are in need of a powerful strategy for building people up without tearing them down. Whereas Part I of this book focuses on the destructive power of organizations, Part V provides strategies for you to transform your organization, your community, and your world. The rest of the book is the very best of the book. In Parts II-IV, you will create your leadership journey and legacy, gain the skills you need to be successful in that journey, and learn to overcome your foes, your fears, and your failures.

In 2008, I picked up a book that dramatically changed my thinking and the trajectory of my work: *The Lucifer Effect* by Philip Zimbardo. In the first fifteen chapters, Zimbardo describes the situational and social forces that compel average people to do evil things, which helped me understand my own experience with hazing in my organization. In the last chapter, he makes a persuasive case that if we can compel average people to do evil things, can't we also make average people do *heroic* things?

At about the same time, I was introduced to the documentary *Finding Joe*, directed by Patrick Takaya Solomon. It's a film about mythologist Joseph Campbell and his study of the hero's journey. More importantly, it inspires people to make their own hero journeys. For the last sixteen years, I have been coaching, mentoring, and teaching hundreds, if not thousands, of people in their own journeys. I hold several certifications, including as a Board Certified Coach by the Center for

Credentialing and Education, Inc. and as a Gallup-Certified Strengths Coach. In 2007, I was honored to be named an Anti-Hazing Hero by HazingPrevention.Org, and in 2010, I was recognized as one of two Outstanding Greek Life Professionals by the Fraternity Information and Programming Group (FIPG). In 2018, I was recognized by the students of the Carlson School of Management as Staff of the Year.

I know choosing to confront a culture of hazing or going on your own leadership journey can be intimidating, if not downright scary. I've been there, too. It is easy and safe to live a life inside the norm, but it is also less fulfilling and meaningful. When we choose what is familiar and what is safe for our lives, we forfeit a life that is meaningful and significant. We miss out on the opportunity to make a difference with our lives.

A Lakota parable shared by Joseph Marshall in the book *The Lakota Way* says every one of us has two choices before us. The first is the Red Road, which is difficult, treacherous, twisting, and filled with obstacles. The second is the Black Road, which is smooth, wide, and well-traveled. One of these roads will bring you purpose and peace; the other will bring you comfort and ease. The choice is always yours.

If you choose to embark on this journey with me, I am here for you. I want to be your coach and your mentor, and I promise to guide you along the path and be with you every step along the way.

Are you ready to challenge the status quo? Are you ready to confront your fears? Are you ready to change your organization, your community, and most of all, your own life?

If you are ready to find the hero inside of you, let's begin our journey together.

PART I
EMERGING FROM HAZING

"Heroism begins with each person considering, internalizing, and shaping his or her mission."

— Chris Lowney

CHAPTER 1
EXPERIENCING HAZING

"Our sense of power is more vivid when we break a man's
spirit than when we win his heart."

— Eric Hoffer

A broken spirit.

It's a depressing way to start, isn't it? But isn't that, in fact, where many
of us are?

After all, how many of us are on our way to becoming the best versions
of ourselves?

In February 2018, Gallup and Sharecare released the 2017 results
from the Gallup-Sharecare Well-Being Index, which measures the
overall wellbeing of people living in the United States. In 2017, the
national score fell from 62.1 (out of 100) in 2016 to 61.5, marking the
largest year-over-year decline since the index began in 2008. Roughly one-quarter of the US population is not thriving in any of the five
areas of wellbeing, and another quarter is thriving in only one of the
five areas, which include: Purpose, Social, Financial, Physical, and
Community.

The index's larger-than-ever tumble was led by its largest falls in two of the five dimensions of wellbeing: Purpose Wellbeing (liking what you do each day and being motivated to achieve your goals) and Social Wellbeing (having supportive relationships and love in your life), which include our daily activities and work, as well as the people we interact with every day.

We are not satisfied by how we spend our time and whom we spend that time with.

What is going on in our groups, organizations, and teams?

According to Gallup's State of the Global Workplace report in 2017, 85 percent of employees are not engaged or are actively disengaged at work. Less than two out of every ten employees is thriving in the workplace.

If we look at these two research studies together, it is easy to come to the conclusion that our organizations are prohibiting us from becoming the best versions of ourselves. In fact, for many of us, they are tearing us down.

We are no longer looking up at our goals but looking down at our feet. We want to speak out and stand up for the causes, issues, and people we care about, but instead, we sit down and shut up. We are surviving rather than thriving.

But it does not have to be that way. We *can* change ourselves and our organizations.

From 1998 to 2000, I was broken by my organization, too. However, in my case, it was done on purpose. In fact, we were told over and over again that we would be "torn down" in order to be "built back up again." The lessons I learned from that experience, although dramatic, have proven invaluable in understanding how groups, organizations, and teams are failing to provide the skills, strategies, and tools for each and every one of us to become the best versions of ourselves.

In this chapter, I will share my experience in a hazing organization with you. In Chapters 2 and 3, we will look at how those psychological, situational, and social forces were tearing down rather than building up. Then, beginning in Part II, we will embark on our journey to become the best versions of ourselves, and building the cultures, structures, and systems to transform ourselves and our organizations. In Part III, you will begin a series of tests through which you will acquire the six Heroic Arts, which will lead you to success in your journey. Then, in Part IV, you will not only confront your foes, your fears, and your failures, but you will overcome them. Finally, in Part V, you will receive the skills, strategies, and tools for transforming your organization, your community, and your world.

IN A BASEMENT ON CAMPUS

At the beginning of the week, twenty-four college students descended into a basement that for them became the bowels of hell. They were dehumanized, humiliated, and ultimately broken. The process began with the stripping of their clothes, their identities, and their privacy. It ended after six days with their dignity, humanity, and wellbeing having been taken away. In between, the students were awoken repeatedly throughout the nights, were forced to simulate sexual acts with others, and had bathroom and eating privileges restricted.

The words above could describe a hazing practice at any high school or college, for any athletic team, fraternity, marching band, sorority, or any other organization any of us may seek to join. But, in fact, they describe the landmark Stanford Prison Experiment in 1971. Prior to the experiment, Philip Zimbardo and associates meticulously screened a group of students at Stanford University. On all emotional and psychological measures, the students scored between the fortieth and sixtieth percentiles; they were average people.

The students were randomly assigned to be either guards or prisoners. The experiment was scheduled for fourteen days, but in less than a week, the guards had become so sadistic and the prisoners so submissive, that the experiment was halted for the safety and wellbeing of everyone involved.

What caused a group of average college students to internalize and radicalize their roles in such a brief period? And what does the Stanford Prison Experiment have to do with hazing practices?

Whether an organization fails to build up its members because of hazing or another form of organizational dysfunction, it is common for defenders of the organization to repeat the well-known saying, "A few bad apples spoil the barrel," meaning a few bad individuals are responsible for bad behaviors.

But one of the most important findings of the Stanford Prison Experiment is that a bad barrel can spoil the apples inside, and a closer look at hazing will show that, as well.

Even if your organization does not have a culture of hazing, the dynamics and forces that contribute to that culture can be present in subtle and not-so-subtle ways in any dysfunctional or struggling organization.

Fraternities and sororities, based on their founding principles and missions, ought to be immune from such dangerous and destructive practices. Beginning in 1776, college students, who were not altogether different from those today, forged the idea that we know now as fraternities.

As that idea was being conceived, those founders believed if the idea was successful, it would create a long-lasting movement that would feed the hungry, give clothes to the poor, and provide comfort and medicine to the sick, all while providing life-changing experiences to the people within the movement.

For this reason, these organizations are called "social" organizations. Their core mission, that is, their deepest purpose, was to serve society.

Throughout the founding histories of fraternities and sororities, you will find a group of people who endeavored to create organizations that would transform their members, and through the transformation of those members, uplift their communities, country, and the world.

Unfortunately, in many places, that idea is failing, and if organizations with such noble beginnings can fail in this way, what organization possibly could be immune to such powerful forces?

HAZING IS ADDICTIVE

On September 14, 2017, Louisiana State University became the site of at least the 221st possible hazing death in US history, according to data provided by hazing researcher Hank Nuwer. The eighteen-year-old student, Maxwell Raymond Gruver, was taken to a hospital from the Phi Delta Theta fraternity house at Louisiana State's campus a few hours before because of a "medical emergency." Gruber was later pronounced dead, and the episode was being investigated as a "potential hazing incident."

Since 1961, at least one person at a United States school has died each year from hazing according to information tracked by Nuwer at HankNuwer.com.

Similarly, according to data maintained by HazingPrevention.Org, forty-four of the fifty US states have laws against hazing, and most, if not all, colleges and universities in the United States also have policies prohibiting hazing.

With an overwhelming amount of evidence on the consequences of hazing, why does this practice persist? Why, when there are so many reasons for so many people to know better, do those people not *do* better?

When individuals have behavioral problems connected to illegal activities that often end in imprisonment or death, we may assume they are suffering from an addiction to a controlled substance.

In the case of hazing, many are suffering from an addiction, and their organizations are their de facto dealers. As you will see, the psychological, situational, and social forces at work are incredibly powerful ones.

In *The Lucifer Effect*, Zimbardo described how, as evidenced by his landmark research study, the Stanford Prison Experiment, powerful social forces can alter the behavior of ordinary people. In the experiment, good people playing the role of guards suddenly became perpetrators of evil, while others playing the role of prisoners became submissive victims as a result of the powerful situational and social forces acting on them.

As human beings, we tend to believe that good people do good things, whereas bad people do bad things. The Stanford Prison Experiment demonstrated that the context of the situation is important, and that the line between good and evil is more pliable than we realize. It is possible for social settings to exert a significant force on the behavior and mental functioning of both individuals and groups.

In *The Lucifer Effect*, Zimbardo is careful to point out that individuals are not absolved of their actions, but in creating positive changes in human behavior, it is important to understand the effects of situational, social, and systemic forces.

I know firsthand, having experienced hazing as a college student, that those forces begin small, but their momentum is unmistakable.

For me, it began with euphoria, exhilaration, and a feeling of freedom. Whatever apprehension I felt, it had dissipated by the time my feet glided through the courtyard between the first two sororities on our route.

As far as I knew, the event was entirely spontaneous. Only a few seconds before, as most of my pledge class was standing around on the first floor of the fraternity house during our first night, one of the sophomores came bounding down the stairs completely naked. As he reached the last few feet before the already open door, he waved his arm and beckoned, "Let's go!"

Before the twenty or so of us had a chance to give it a second thought, our clothes were strewn throughout the entryway and we were on our way. We weaved among a half-dozen fraternity and sorority houses, making our way to the municipal fountains just beyond the campus' border. After a quick dip in the fountain, we ran as fast as we could back to the house.

While still 100 feet away from the house, I saw the unmistakable silhouette of a police officer, flashlight in hand, standing at the top of the stairs leading back into the house. The officer's flashlight followed each of us as we passed through the open door, racing into the house and up the stairs to conceal our identities.

I don't remember any consequences of this act, despite the fact that the police obviously had direct knowledge of the activity—just that we'd had our first taste of the hazing that was in store for us.

We were hooked. The situational, social, and systemic forces that Zimbardo had described had their foothold, and the momentum of those forces was now mounting.

After saying "yes" to the first hazing activity, it became easier and easier to continue participating without demonstrating much resistance, even as the behaviors became more dangerous, more embarrassing, and more illegal along the way.

HAZING IS INSIDIOUS

Although "line ups" and other pledge class activities occurred at least every other week, the first week of our second semester brought a whole new low. For the entirety of the first semester, the actual schedule and timeline of our pledging was hidden from us. We had no idea what was coming our way.

Thus, when the older members came running into our sleeping dorm, banging pots and pans, blowing horns, and screaming at the tops of their lungs in the early hours of one January morning, we knew Hell Week had arrived.

We were given a new, stricter set of rules, including a ban on the use of caffeine and nicotine, and we were forbidden from using the front door. We were also made to engage in some sort of menial activity before finally being allowed to go to bed in the wee hours of the morning.

After only a few hours, we were again summoned to the basement by a cacophony of pots and pans for a line up, where we were informed that the last twenty-four hours of torture had, in fact, been "Fake Hell Week" rather than the real deal.

The worst was yet to come, and our fear was very real.

Now that our pledge class knew the following week would be the real Hell Week, we planned our pledge sneak for the coming weekend. This was a road trip for the new members and a couple of older members who would buy alcohol for us—a little respite before the final trial.

But not everybody was able to let go.

Following a 400-mile drive in matching fifteen-passenger vans, crisscrossing the tundra of the upper Midwest in early January, all but two members of our thirty-person pledge class gleefully raced into the casino when we arrived, leaving Flounder and I in one of the vans.

As I sat in the front passenger seat, I could see giant tears rolling down my friend Flounder's face as he was seated behind the driver's wheel. Flounder, a big-hearted friend who had earned his nickname based on his resemblance to the character from *Animal House*, described to me how he had been made fun of his entire life.

"When I joined this fraternity, I thought I had finally found a group of guys who would accept me for who I am," he said, sobbing.

At that moment, we resolved we would endure Hell Week and then do our best to change the fraternity's culture once we gained full membership.

The following week was the real Hell Week.

HAZING IS DESTRUCTIVE

In addition to the reinstatement of the rules that had been instituted for Fake Hell Week, we had to wear plain white T-shirts whenever we were inside the house. Many of the T-shirts bore degrading insults or homophobic phrases scribbled across them by the older members or had huge chunks of fabric cut out to fat-shame any of the larger men in our pledge class.

On the back of the T-shirts, we were forced to write the numbers one through twenty. Then we were told that, at any time or for any reason, one of the older members could cross off any number of those digits. When the last number was crossed off, the T-shirt's wearer would be kicked out of the fraternity immediately. We were also called "wops," and when one of us dared ask why we would be known by that particular phrase, one of the older members said it was the sound a 200-pound sack of shit makes when it's thrown out of a third-story window.

Other than the older members' impish delight in arbitrarily eliminating numbers from the backs of our T-shirts, the most common way we lost points was by not caring for our "baby," a raw egg we were required to take care of for the entire week. Not surprisingly, the greatest threats to our babies were the older members themselves, who gained some sort of sadistic thrill from throwing our eggs against the wall. Each time the wall gained a fresh coat of yolk, we were told we could salvage the membership of the person whose egg was obliterated by deep cleaning the entire house.

Needless to say, the house was extraordinarily clean that week.

Throughout the week, we were sent on convenience store runs to buy chewing tobacco, cigarettes, beverages, or anything else the older members requested from us.

At meal times, we were forced to feed our pledge brothers facing backwards on our chairs with our arms protruding between the supports in the backs of the chairs. Following each meal, any leftovers were scraped into an army surplus-sized pot, where they were intermingled with cigarette butts, saliva, and who knows what else.

When "lights out" mercifully arrived at the end of each grueling day, we were finally allowed to go to sleep around two in the morning, with the caveat that we had to learn to sleep with "Ring of Fire" by Johnny Cash blaring at full volume in our sleeping dorm.

HAZING IS SYSTEMATIC

Day by day, we were systematically and thoroughly torn down. Beginning with the smallest step away from who we were and what we normally would or would not do, we were conditioned to accept larger and larger deviations from our former selves and our long-held principles.

From streaking to cleaning one of the older member's rooms, we soon found ourselves doing some things I still have not publicly disclosed, but unfortunately, will never forget.

On the final day of Hell Week, we were awoken after even less sleep than we had had the previous nights. We began the morning with a round of calisthenics. Then the senior members brought in a whole bunch of very cheap and very warm beer that we were told we had to consume all of that morning. Meanwhile, we were ordered to pretend we were play-by-play announcers commentating on every scene of a pornographic movie the seniors had purchased.

That night, we were again shaken from our slumbers in the now normal way, but this time we were quickly shown into one of the other sleeping dorms. There was a sense of panic in the older members' voices. They told us someone from the fraternity's national office had arrived, so they had to initiate us quickly. They shoved a box of condoms at us and instructed us to hurry up and put them on.

Blindfolded, we were then guided to the basement one by one for what we were told was the final ritual, where we would demonstrate our commitment to the fraternity.

Fortunately, there was no reason for the condom, and the final tests we endured while blindfolded were only verbal ones.

Once each of us had completed this test, we were taken to a third room, so as not to spoil the true nature of the test for the others still waiting.

After every one of us completed his test, we were reassembled in the shape of a horseshoe in the basement, the now standard formation for line-ups. The older members brought the army surplus-sized pot downstairs from the kitchen and told us we had to consume a full glass of the concoction in order to prove one final time that we would "do anything for the fraternity."

As we were again being blindfolded, overflowing cups of the foul mixture were waved beneath our noses. When all of the blindfolds were in place, cups were placed in our hands. We were told to toast to the fraternity and then immediately consume the cup's entire contents.

I opened my throat as far as possible, allowing the liquid to cascade down. I don't know whether or not I actually tasted the liquid, but the celebration that ensued revealed that the pot's contents had been substituted at the last possible moment with cups of cold beer.

When the celebratory cloud of initiation and the fog of prolonged sleep deprivation had cleared, I began reflecting on how I had subjected myself to a half year of smoldering harassment and a week of white-hot emotional, physical, psychological, and sexual abuse.

But to what end? Had I become a better person, or had I merely sacrificed my dignity, my integrity, and my principles?

EXERCISE

In what ways does your group, organization, or team inhibit the growth of its members, either actively or passively tearing them down?

_____

_____

_____

_____

In what ways does your organization empower its members to become the best versions of themselves?

_____

_____

_____

_____

SUMMARY

Hazing is a disease in many organizations, attacking and subverting the very best of what those organizations can be. Then why does it continue, maybe even growing and spreading? Hazing is addictive, beginning with permissible pranks and stunts, which form its insidious foundation. As the hazing becomes less and less "innocent," it simultaneously becomes more and more dangerous and destructive, but the psychological, situational, and social momentum combine with systemic forces to make it more and more difficult for participants to stop the then-runaway train.

CHAPTER 2

EXPOSING HAZING

"The line between good and evil is in the center
of every human heart."

— Aleksandr Solzhenitsyn

In the last chapter, we discussed what is probably a common experience with hazing.

Experiences with hazing not altogether different from my own probably occur on countless campuses throughout the country every year. After all, nobody was hospitalized or killed, and nobody was imprisoned. But that certainly does not make the experience a positive one for us or for the organization as a whole.

These powerful psychological, situational, and social forces are not limited to fraternities, sororities, athletic teams, marching bands, and any other organizations where hazing may occur. They can appear in subtle and not-so-subtle ways in any organization, team, or workplace.

Whenever we have a goal of bringing new people into our organizations and providing a process through which they can become the best possible members, we must ensure that the process will develop them in positive and productive ways.

But more than that, in every organization, we have the opportunity to create cultures that empower each and every person to become the best version of him- or herself. By doing so, we have the power to transform not only our organizations, but our communities and our world, as well.

In this chapter, we will examine the psychological, situational, and social forces behind hazing, exposing all of the ways it falls short of its lofty, oft-repeated promises as a successful onboarding process for many organizations.

HAZING IS A BROKEN PROMISE

Hazing promised me big things.

Hazing promised to forge lifelong friendships with my fraternity brothers.

Hazing promised to provide positive character traits, such as integrity, respect, and responsibility.

Hazing promised to tear me down, only to make me stronger.

Every one of these promises was broken or left unfulfilled.

However, most of all, hazing promised to make me a man.

Of all of the promises that hazing made to me and numerous other people throughout the world, this was the greatest lie of them all.

The truth is, in addition to its dangerous and debaucherous elements, hazing causes adults to become children.

Today, as a father of two boys, I have seen how children develop, first from infants into toddlers, and then from toddlers into school-aged children.

Likewise, as a professional, I have worked with eighteen to twenty-two-year-olds since 2002, including in roles as a fraternity house director, professional fraternity and sorority advisor, academic advisor, and career coach.

I also possess an advanced degree in counseling and personal development. As a result of all of that education and my day-to-day experiences, I know one of the most important transitions that each of us must make as we mature from children to adults is the transition from a "me-centered" existence to a "we-driven" one.

As infants, we shook our caregivers countless times from their slumbers. They strove to meet our most pressing needs, regardless of how sick, stressed out, or tired they may have been.

As we grew from infants to children and then from adolescents to adults, one of our most important developmental tasks is to develop mature interpersonal relationships, which are described as not only freedom from narcissism and self-centeredness but also a shift from dependence or dominance toward interdependence among equals.

Hazing is, at its foundation, an act of dominance and power, as well as a demonstration of immaturity. After all, one of the most common excuses in support of hazing is some variation of the cliché that "boys will be boys."

As a pledge, a member, an alumnus, and a professional, I have seen many young men and women who became caricatures and immature, reckless imitations of their true selves, despite knowing that many of them would not acknowledge those darker, more juvenile versions of their selves in any public way. They were ashamed of who they were and what they had done when their hazing practices were exposed.

Hazing became a way for these people to act out ego-feeding, self-centered roles, without any concern for consequences or any reflection on whom they "really are." They did not have to worry about how they might be perceived by others, both inside and outside of their organizations, because they were merely carrying out a role prescribed to them as members of their organizations. They blindly accepted that those behaviors reflected how members of their organizations acted.

If those who complete the hazing process regress to less mature and more reckless stages of human development, isn't it obvious that hazing is failing to fulfill its promises of building better people?

Why then does hazing continue to exist, and how does it manipulate not only its victims, but its perpetrators as well?

HAZING IS DYSFUNCTIONAL

Hazing persists because it does, in fact, meet some fundamental human needs, albeit in obviously destructive and dysfunctional ways.

If you were to ask people about their motivations for hazing, what do you think they would say? The most common responses often include some combination of a desire for bonding, for instilling discipline, for proving one's self, for showing respect for the organization, and for possessing a mechanism for ensuring that only the best individuals become members of our organizations.

Let's examine each of these five motives.

1. Bonding
Look back at a few of the hardest and most painful moments of your life. Who was with you? What kinds of relationships do you have with those people now? You may have formed extraordinarily strong bonds with the people who experienced those hardships with you.

We can form a truly unique bond with those with whom we share the hardest, most difficult experiences. Psychologists refer to this as the severity-affiliation-attraction hypothesis, which means that human beings tend to bond with the people with whom they go through traumatic experiences.

But this does not mean that those people necessarily bond to the people who are inflicting those traumatic experiences on them. In fact, they may never truly forgive those who hazed them.

Those who do bond with those who hazed them are conditioning their brains to conflate affection with affliction. In that process, they are training themselves to accept torment and torture in place of compassion and love. This situation is commonly known as "Stockholm Syndrome." It develops when people are in such dire situations that they have to rely on the person who abuses them for their survival. Compliance and subjugation become mechanisms for survival, as well as substitutions for genuine, positive interpersonal relationships.

In hazing environments, aren't those who are hazed likewise reliant on their hazers for their survival, whether a very real physical survival or a metaphorical social survival in which they are allowed to continue as members of the organization?

Is inflicting psychological violence the way we want to construct and continue our organizations? What are the lasting effects on our members as they leave our organizations and continue their lives? What is the larger lasting effect on our society?

2. Discipline
Some people will defend hazing as a disciplinary process, or a program through which the newest members acquire positive skills such as organization, time management, and work ethic.

In my experience, the high level of discipline demanded during my own six-month pledging process disappeared as quickly as the evidence of the hazing activities themselves. The men who were pushed hardest regressed the quickest. As soon as they reached the "finish line" of initiation and became full members of the organization, the cleanliness of their rooms, the quality of their academic performance, and the timeliness of their membership and housing payments trailed off.

In other words, the discipline lasted only as long as the punishment. For those members, the discipline they showed during pledging was a result of an influx of stress chemicals in the brain, rather than the result of an intrinsic motivation they could tap into on their own. Long-term, they also are conditioning their brains to need that same level of stress in order to prompt performance. In this way, hazing organizations are inhibiting, rather than promoting, the type of behavior they desire.

3. Proving Yourself
One of the most oft-cited boasts of hazing organizations is that hazing instills leadership skills. Despite the frequency of its citation as a result, this point may be the easiest one to refute.

By any definition of the term, leadership requires being the first person to lead the way and to step forward, particularly in difficult situations.

In all of those line-ups I participated in, one of the most persistent characteristics was that the first person who voiced any opposition or reluctance was punished the most severely. The first person to step up was the first to be knocked back down.

Instead of teaching people to demonstrate leadership by stepping up, we were being taught to sit down and shut up. Instead of exercising and growing our leadership skills, pledging became a six-month Whack-A-Mole game where our pledge class played the role of the pummeled rodents.

4. Respect
It is a long-held and cherished cliché that we value those things we work hardest for. Thomas Paine, a philosopher, political activist, revolutionary, and one of the Founding Fathers of the United States, once observed, "What we obtain too cheap, we esteem too lightly."

A case can be made that we cherish and value those things for which we work the hardest, a concept referred to as "justification of effort" by psychologists. This idea refers to the phenomenon by which, when we are subjected to a traumatic experience, our minds seek to justify that experience by saying the experience itself fulfilled a larger purpose.

Many of us who have gone through a hazing process may say, "I went through some truly awful hazing, which means my membership in that organization is truly special."

It is clear this type of respect for the organization may be effective, but it is still flawed by nature.

And what about respect for the older members of the organization?

In my experience, the greatest proponents of hazing were also the ones who, almost exclusively, were the least involved in the day-to-day operations of the organization. I cannot tell you how many older members I met for the first time at line-ups and during Hell Week, or how many of those members I never saw again once Hell Week was over.

5. The Best of the Best

If your organization cannot attract the best and brightest, and has to rely on hazing either to eliminate weaker new members or somehow strengthen those who choose to join, doesn't that point to a larger problem about the quality of that organization and its membership?

In addition, the field of psychology suggests that some of the critical factors involved in hazing not only limit an organization's ability to build up its members but may, in fact, turn them to a darker path. According to Philip Zimbardo in *The Lucifer Effect*, there are five factors that compel ordinary people to do evil things. It is not a coincidence that all five of those factors also are present in most hazing organizations, given how dangerous and even deadly hazing has been for so many people over such a long period of time.

Authority: A separation of newer members and older members according to an arbitrary set of roles and rules. Example (from my hazing experience): Pledge rules.

Deindividuation: Costumes, darkness, and other devices that promote anonymity. Example (from my hazing experience): Dimming of lights during hazing activities or wearing identity-concealing masks.

Dehumanization: The minimization of a victim's humanity. Example (from my hazing experience): Referring to pledges as "wops." Again, "wop" being the sound of a 200-pound sack of shit hitting the pavement.

Sleep deprivation and time perspective: The disruption of sleep and imposition of tedious activities, which limit the ability of the victim to maintain a sense of identity beyond the current setting. Example (from my hazing experience): Playing Johnny Cash's "Ring of Fire" at a high volume over and over throughout the night.

Social approval: A need for acceptance and to be a team player. Example (from my hazing experience): Lifting up as exemplars the pledges who followed the rules, kept their mouths shut, and maintained a low profile.

By addressing each of these five factors identified by Zimbardo at individual, peer, group, institutional, community, and societal levels, we can effectively push back and prevent a culture of hazing. Our efforts also must include prevention, early intervention, and response strategies to be successful in challenging cultures of hazing. We cannot begin and end by responding to incidents, injuries, or reports of hazing; we must include initiatives for intervening early in hazing situations and for stopping hazing behaviors altogether. Prevention efforts can create safer environments and target underlying causes, and early intervention efforts can empower us to speak out about "little h" hazing before it becomes "big H" hazing.

In order to implement positive, transformative prevention strategies, our organizations need people who believe a better way exists to deliver experiences that meet our fundamental human needs and who are empowered and equipped to implement those experiences.

Finding and empowering these people is our escape plan for overcoming cultures that tear people down rather than build them up.

EXERCISE

Consider how your organization exhibits the five factors identified by Zimbardo. List examples for each of the five factors.

Authority: _____

_____

_____

Deindividuation: _____

_____

_____

Dehumanization: _____

_____

_____

Sleep deprivation and time perspective: _____

_____

_____

Social approval: _____

_____

_____

SUMMARY

As we enter and continue our participation in groups, organizations, and teams, there are five natural and neutral desires that can drive our behaviors and choices, including the desire to bond, to demonstrate and instill discipline, to prove ourselves, to give and receive respect, and to want only the best people to be part of our organizations. In any destructive or dysfunctional organization, and in particular those with cultures of hazing, these very big promises are left unfulfilled. In each and every way, hazing organizations are falling short.

CHAPTER 3

ESCAPING HAZING

"Do not believe in anything simply because you have heard it. Do not believe in anything simply because it is spoken and rumored by many.... Do not believe in traditions because they have been handed down for many generations. But after observation and analysis, when you find that anything agrees with reason and is conducive to the good and benefit of one and all, then accept it and live up to it."

— Buddha

In the previous chapter, we identified five common defenses or motives for engaging in hazing: A combination of a desire for bonding, for instilling discipline, an opportunity to prove one's self, demonstrating respect for the organization, and a mechanism for ensuring that only the best become members of our organizations.

On the surface, are any of those five motives evil or harmful in and of themselves? The answer is clearly "no." In fact, each of those motivations is natural and neutral, and you will find people who desire these same things in every organization. These motives are neither positive nor negative. For this reason, they also are core components in historical and traditional rites of passage. All of us crave challenging and meaningful experiences in our lives.

Rites of passage can be seen as symbolic and theatrical onboarding processes for organizations and communities. In order for a young person to transition into a leadership position in those groups, he or she often participates in a rite of passage. From this perspective, rites of passage are simply developmental processes that facilitate an individual's growth.

The basic components of a rite of passage include: separation, initiation, and return phases. We can find these same components in the stories and mythologies we share.

For example, in the Harry Potter book series, Harry learns he is a wizard, leaves the Dursleys, undergoes an initiation into the wizarding world and its unique threats at Hogwarts School of Witchcraft and Wizardry, and then returns to the Dursleys each summer.

As a second example, in *The Wizard of Oz*, Dorothy is separated from her home in Kansas, comes face to face with her own doubts and insecurities in the Land of Oz, and finally learns that she already possesses the power to return to her home in Kansas.

MEETING OUR NEEDS

It is no coincidence that formal rites of passage follow the very same formula as those we read in books or see in theaters and on TV.

In the separation phase of traditional rites of passage, initiates are often physically removed from their families, their homes, and their normal roles. This is a signal to the community and to the initiates themselves that they are going through a period of transformation.

When used in hazing organizations, the separation phase is often accomplished by limiting contact with non-members and by using special roles and rules exclusively for new members, which points back to the difference in power that Philip Zimbardo observed in the Stanford Prison Experiment.

All too often, this separation is used as a weapon against the new members and as a shield for the hazing organization, rather than as an incubator that facilitates the new member's growth and transformation.

Then, as initiates enter the initiation phase of a traditional rite of passage, they go through emotional, physical, and psychological challenges. The challenge's purpose is not to punish or tear down the initiates, but rather to provide an opportunity for them to grow their confidence and skills to new levels and rise.

When we examine the initiation phase in hazing organizations, too often the new members are harassed, ridiculed, and subjugated by the older members, and the challenges presented to them often include violent or illegal activities that have little or no connection to the purpose of the organization they are joining.

Why, then, is a clear, positive purpose imperative to a productive and successful rite of passage?

As initiates reach the end of the initiation phase and prepare for their return, having exhausted themselves through that process, they must reflect on what that experience means for them and their future sense of self. This is the threshold between the initiation and the return.

In productive and successful rites of passage, the challenges presented in the initiation phase are others-centered and purposeful. The rites prepare the new member to care and provide for others, rather than merely "making it through" a period of punishment and subjugation.

When initiates reflect on and seek the larger meaning of a productive rite of passage, it is self-evident throughout the process because the initiation's endeavors reflect the process' goals, which allows the initiate to embrace the larger purpose of the process and the organization.

But in hazing organizations, the experience's larger meaning is absent or obscured, resulting in a state of cognitive dissonance and confusion. When a clear purpose is absent, the initiate's mind will determine that the experience itself is the larger purpose, a phenomenon psychologists call the "justification of effort."

If the experience itself, the hazing process, assumes a place in the initiate's mind as the purpose and value of the experience, a culture of hazing that counters and undermines the organization's larger purpose is born. Through this process, hazing then becomes a substitute for the organization and the ritual's true purpose.

During the return phase of traditional rites of passage, new members are wholly accepted as full members because they have proven they possess the skills and values necessary to serve in the role of elder, protector, and provider in their communities.

In hazing organizations, new members are accepted as full members simply by virtue of "making it through" or surviving a series of tasks that are disconnected from the organization's larger purpose. Absent a clear role connected to the organization's purpose, the possession of this new identity as full members in a hazing organization also confers on the new members the duty to continue the hazing tradition.

To say that hazing organizations follow the rites of passage phases during an initiation is no different than completing a paint-by-number landscape and calling yourself an artist.

While hazing processes possess the basic outline of productive and successful rites of passage, they lack the details and development-focused delivery that make true rites of passage successful in building better people.

The focus in hazing organizations is on tearing down, rather than building up.

At its core, a transformative experience is a self-upgrade. In the beginning, a particular idea or skill is not part of who you are. Afterward, however, it becomes part of who you are because you have been changed as a direct result of the transformational experience.

THE RIGHT WAYS TO DO RITES OF PASSAGE

In his book, *Adam's Return*, Richard Rohr outlines the five right ways to create meaningful, transformative rites of passage: Strength through Struggle, Strength through Service, Strength through Sacrifice, Strength through Support, and Strength through Transformation. Let's look at each one in detail.

Strength Through Struggle: Managing One's Emotions

Allow me to be clear: If you hurt people during an initiation or rite of passage, you are doing it all wrong. But that does not mean that the experience cannot be challenging. At the experience's conclusion, the initiates should be exhausted from their labor, but that labor must serve a larger purpose.

As adolescents become adults, it is important that they learn how to do things that are emotionally and/or physically demanding. For example, children often allow emotions such as anger or fear to drive them to fight. However, as adults, one of our most important developmental tasks is to learn to control and direct our emotions; we learn to fight at the most opportune times and only for those things worth fighting for. Arthur Chickering referred to this developmental task as "managing one's emotions."

Strength Through Service: Developing Mature Interpersonal Relationships

The second developmental task present in rites of passage is to develop mature interpersonal relationships, characterized by a freedom from focusing only on ourselves and a shift from dependence or dominance toward interdependence between equals.

We, as human beings, are first and foremost social beings.

If we fail to have meaningful, purposeful relationships in concert with others, we fail to live up to our purpose as social beings.

If we cannot respect others, we cannot respect ourselves.

If we cannot demonstrate our compassion and guidance for the initiates in our care, we cannot provide them with an effective rite of passage.

In our world, it is all too common and easy to find faults, to knock others down, or to respond with a sarcastic or superficial thought. Reactions like these take so little effort that we can spout them without even thinking.

On the other hand, it is challenging to give from our strength, to lift others up, and to reach deep inside ourselves to offer others the depth, encouragement, and support they—and we ourselves—need.

Our world is dominated by leaders who would prefer to win at all costs, rather than to find a common ground and a shared purpose with their ideological opponents. Is it any wonder that the rest of us cannot find the courage and strength to believe in others? Where are our examples?

Strength Through Sacrifice: Developing Purpose

The third principle builds on the principle of becoming others-centered and "strength through service." When we connect in meaningful and purposeful ways with others, we take the next step by becoming responsible for someone or for something else.

One of the defining characteristics of assuming a leadership role, whether in your community, in your organization, or even in your own family, is becoming responsible for others, whether children, partners, or our own parents. To put it a different way, if everything you do is for you, how does your purpose differ from that of a small child who seeks to fulfill only her/his own needs, regardless of the effect on others?

This principle reflects the developmental task of developing purpose. In short, there is a level of responsibility and self-discipline that comes when you realize someone else is counting on you.

Ask yourself:
- How would my world be different if others looked at me and saw my greatest potential?
- How would the world be different if I looked at others and gave of myself so they could reach their greatest potential?

Strength Through Support: Establishing Identity

In a contemporary rite of passage, it is not only necessary for you to learn to listen, learn from, and honor others with authority or experience, but also to align your journey with the learnings of others.

In a productive and successful rite of passage, mentors guide initiates, equipping them with the physical and psychological tools to continue and complete their journeys. The initiates honor and respect the mentors and the insights they share, but ultimately, they align those lessons with the initiates' own unique journeys.

By aligning your journey with the lessons you learn along the way, you can handle criticism and feedback from others, having developed the skill of articulating and solidifying one's own values, part of Chickering's developmental task of establishing identity.

Strength Through Transformation: Developing Integrity

The fifth and final component is illustrated by a quote by Friedrich Nietzsche, "The snake that cannot shed its skin perishes."

This does not, of course, refer to a physical death, but a transformation. In the final stage of the initiation, the initiate experiences a symbolic death, and a new adult emerges.

We understand that through our challenges, frustrations, setbacks, or triumphs, we develop, we grow, and we become stronger. When we break through and succeed despite those obstacles, we are in fact building skills and an improved sense of self that we can call upon again in the future. In this way, this principle parallels Chickering's developmental task of developing integrity.

EXERCISE

For each of the "Strength through…" components of productive and successful rites of passage, consider how well your organization does in fulfilling that developmental need. Then, mark the corresponding score on the item's scale, where 1 = Not at all and 5 = Completely, could not do any better. Finally, make notes beneath each scale indicating why you chose that particular score.

Strength through Struggle: 1 2 3 4 5

Strength through Service: 1 2 3 4 5

Strength through Sacrifice: 1 2 3 4 5

Strength through Support: 1 2 3 4 5

Strength through Transformation: 1 2 3 4 5

HAZING OFFERS NO MIDDLE GROUND

An awful lot of people are asking an awful lot of hard questions in the aftermath of an ever-climbing number of hazing-related deaths, and Timothy Piazza's death on February 4, 2017, at the Beta Theta Pi fraternity house at Pennsylvania State University, in particular, has shaken a lot of people's assumptions about protecting people from such tragedies.

The alumni, the chapter, and the university employed every best practice in the hazing prevention playbook: Alcohol-free housing? Check. Live-in advisor? Check. Award-winning educational programs? Check. Security cameras? Check.

But those measures were not enough—not even close. If it were possible to create a physical environment that was hazing-proof, you could not imagine one much stronger than the one at the Beta Theta Pi fraternity house at Penn State.

Environments, however, are not enough. We need individuals and organizations that are empowered to confront hazing and cultivate heroic leadership.

In a letter released May 12, 2017, by the North-American Interfraternity Conference, Judson Horras, NIC President and CEO, outlined a combustible environment that exists in every hazing organization on any campus:

- Existence of dangerous traditions
- History of substance abuse and hazing in high school
- Proliferation of media glorifying substance abuse and hazing
- Self-preservation in the threat of severe consequences
- Technology that disrupts traditional forms of authority and accountability
- Culture of instant gratification and self-indulgence
- Lack of openness and transparency

There are no easy answers here.

There is only resolve.

We must resolve to create meaningful, positive, and yet challenging, rites of passage. We have the power and the responsibility to instill the courage, skills, and strength that not only protect our members and organizations, but also the power to protect the future of our communities and organizations in increasingly fragmented and turbulent times.

SUMMARY

Hazing fails to connect participants to the larger meaning of the experience that is essential for successful rites of passage. In the absence of that purpose, the experience of hazing itself becomes the larger purpose, effectively replacing the organization's true purpose.

To find success in this fight for the soul of our organizations, we not only need environmental, social, and systemic solutions, but also courageous individuals and groups with the conviction, integrity, and will to lead the way.

PART II
CHALLENGING THE STATUS QUO

"Risk more than others think is safe. Care more than others think is wise. Dream more than others think is practical. Expect more than others think is possible."

— Claude T. Bissell

CHAPTER 4

ANSWERING YOUR CALL

"We must be willing to let go of the life we planned so as to have the life that is waiting for us."

— Joseph Campbell

In the first three chapters, we examined the rites, rituals, and realities of hazing, and we exposed the way hazing falls short of the noble goals and outcomes many people seek through hazing practices.

Now that we know how and why hazing falls short, how do we go about achieving the goals we have for the members of our organizations and delivering positive, powerful, and transformational experiences to them? How do we equip them to be strong, contributing members of our organizations and our communities? Since our goal is to build the best possible groups and teams, what if we begin by building up, rather than by tearing down?

Thankfully, as will be discussed here, we have an instruction manual that is reliable and has been in use throughout human history.

From this manual, we can develop a process that not only limits the possibility of harm to the newest members of our organizations, but also provides them with a rite of passage that empowers them to become the leaders they have the potential to be, the kinds of leaders who can be counted on to stand up against the internal challenges and external threats that any organization, community, or world may face.

In this chapter, we will explore a time-tested process that creates strong bonds among the members of our organizations, develops self-discipline, offers opportunities to prove ourselves, and reaffirms respect for all members of our organizations, as well as providing them with experiences and skills they can draw on for the rest of their lives.

These processes are not only the antidote to hazing, but the elixir to facilitate the greatest growth and development of our members and organizations.

But first, we have to get comfortable with an uncomfortable idea, an idea that has become both cliché and radical. It is cliché because it is seemingly a part of every example and story of finding success by overcoming obstacles. It is a radical idea because, although we have heard this message countless times, very few of us have taken this transformative idea to heart. If we only accepted and acted on this idea, we could literally change the world.

What is this idea? And more importantly, what does it mean for you and for the organization you are part of?

WE SEE IT ON THE SCREEN

In 2017, more than 231 million tickets were sold to just seven of the 730 movies shown on movie screens in the US that year, representing 18.9 percent of the total market share for theatrical releases despite representing less than 1 percent of the total number of theatrical releases. Those movies, including *Wonder Woman, Guardians of the Galaxy Vol. 2, Spider-Man: Homecoming, Thor: Ragnarok, Logan, Justice League, and The Lego Batman Movie* also were seven of the fourteen top-grossing movies of the year.

More than that, you can count on this trend happening year after year.

What did these seven movies have in common? And why are these types of movies so consistently popular year after year, decade after decade?

At the age of ten, at midnight on June 23, 1989, I held in my hand a ticket to the first superhero movie I would see, beginning my own love affair with the genre.

My brother, who is thirteen years older than me, had won a pair of tickets to the midnight premiere of one of the most anticipated movies of my lifetime.

The scene at the movie theater was out of control. The shopping mall where we would see the movie was one of those classic suburban relics, destined to wither away in the new millennium.

But on this night, the lines of people stretched from one end of the pavilion to the other.

By the time we got into the theater, the only remaining seats were in the very first row. Even as a ten-year-old, I remember the strain I felt in my neck most of that night as I stared up at the enormous screen.

It was worth every minute of that strain.

Once the lights dimmed, the previews gave way to the Warner Bros. logo, then the names "Jack Nicholson," "Michael Keaton," and "Kim Basinger" dramatically flew across the screen, and just as the music reached its crescendo, a single word appeared through the darkness:

Batman

Beyond the skill of directors and producers, the talent of actors and actresses, and the technical wonder of special effects, superheroes appeal to generation after generation, breaking box office records on a regular basis.

Have you ever wondered why?

If you were to examine this idea in light of almost any other movie you have seen, or almost any book you have read, you will find a common core. This common core goes beyond "a good story." Maybe surprisingly, it contains an entirely predictable storyline.

In that storyline, the central figures step away from a familiar world or lifestyle. They go on an adventure, where they find some new friends and overcome some obstacles. In the end, they conquer a foe or escape an impossible threat, and then they return to a better version of the familiar world they left.

Despite knowing where the story is going, we buy tickets by the hundreds of millions each year to hear this story told to us again and again.

Why?

Because the story is actually an instructional manual, and the subject of that story is us.

WE SEE OURSELVES IN IT

In 1949, Joseph Campbell, at that time a professor at Sarah Lawrence College, published *The Hero with a Thousand Faces*. As a professor of comparative mythology, Campbell argued that most of the world's great myths, across geography and time, possess a shared single thread, which he referred to as the hero's journey.

Drawing on the psychological work of Abraham Maslow, Sigmund Freud, Stanislav Grof, and in particular, Carl Jung, Campbell discussed how these great myths are present in our consciousness. That is, in the words of Jung, they are archetypes that our brains recognize as common patterns, which can then influence our thoughts and behaviors. They are mental shortcuts that allow us to call upon powerful stories with a short phrase or symbol.

Don't believe me? Imagine using a cleverly disguised trap to gain an opening without alluding to a "Trojan horse," or unleashing innumerable unpredictable outcomes without opening "Pandora's box."

Modern-day superheroes have also found their way into our everyday language with a call for help becoming a flip of the "bat signal." We have even begun replacing traditional Greek heroes for modern ones; history's "Achilles' heel" has become today's "kryptonite."

The power of the hero's journey, however, goes far beyond a handful of turns of phrase. It reverberates deep into who we are and whom we become. It is a seed of potential that exists in each and every one of us, and it is a part of each and every experience we have where we grow and develop.

Whether we are learning to ride a bike or training for a triathlon, changing jobs or preparing for retirement, the hero's journey gives us an instruction manual for the process we will go through: We commit to doing something that is beyond our comfort zone, we encounter people who help us along the way, we experience setbacks and successes, and in the end, we emerge victorious, returning to share our success and inspiration with others.

To describe the stages of the hero's journey with an easy, everyday example, consider a student's first semester in college. I've broken it down into twelve stages:

1. **Status Quo:** Student is attending high school, living at home. This is the student's average, normal, and ordinary world.

2. **Call to adventure:** Student receives admission to college.

3. **Assistance:** Student participates in college orientation, meets academic advisor, classmates, faculty, etc.

4. **Departure:** Student moves onto campus and begins college courses.

5. **Trials:** Student navigates a lot of new things: new freedoms, new friends, new living space, new schedule, etc.

6. **Approach:** Student prepares for first exam.

7. **Crisis:** Student oversleeps day of first exam; awakens in time to throw on some clothes, race across campus, and walk into the classroom, only to find out the test is over. Student receives the lowest possible grade—0 percent.

8. **Treasure:** The instructor reveals to the student that it is still possible not only to pass the class, but to receive an "A" with a high level of work the rest of the semester. Student finds hope, persistence, and resilience.

9. **Result:** Student works hard the rest of the semester and earns an "A."

10. **Return:** Student returns home after the first semester.

11. **New Life:** Student is no longer afraid of failure or setbacks.

12. **Resolution:** Student shares the story of this setback with others, encouraging them to have persistence and resilience.

WE CAN BE HEROES

Although the hero's journey is certainly an instruction manual for any process of change or growth we may go through, its most profound and transformative power comes from the fact that any of us, indeed every single one of us, can be heroes.

But what does it mean to be a hero?

In their article, "The Banality of Heroism," Zeno Franco and Philip Zimbardo write that heroism involves a quest to preserve an ideal/value or life, confronting an actual or anticipated risk/sacrifice, and engaging actively (fight) or passively (resist) in either a one-time act or an ongoing commitment to that quest.

Heroes venture where others have not gone or will not go. Heroes embrace risks or make sacrifices to serve others. Heroes exist in our collective consciousness today in the same way the classical heroes did for the ancients. And heroism is a consistent and constant journey, if not struggle, to go beyond our limits out of a commitment to our own personal values and our compassion for others.

Many of us, however, do not believe we can be heroes. In fact, you may have read that last paragraph and thought, "I could never live up to that definition." You may feel like the luminaries throughout this book—from Tom Burnett, Jr. to Malala Yousafzai—are somehow different from you and me. Unfortunately, many of us do not believe in the potential that exists inside each and every one of us.

The funny thing is, even those who have performed verifiable acts of heroism have said the very same thing. The next time you read a story about or see an interview of someone who has performed an act of heroism, you probably will hear some variation of, "I'm not a hero. I did what anyone else would do."

As a society, we have lifted the label of "hero" out of reach for the very people most often responsible for acts of heroism. For every individual hailed as a hero, you will find countless nameless others who also deserve and have earned that title.

There is a hero in all of us, but few of us accept our call to adventure.

Will you?

WE HEAR THE CALL

At the outset of the hero's journey, the hero-to-be receives a call to adventure or an invitation to depart from the status quo.

In the film *The Matrix*, Neo is awakened from a world that has been pulled over his eyes to blind him from the truth. In the same way, we also have had our eyes and minds drawn to impulse-driven experiences and away from more meaningful and purposeful existences.

The comfortable environment we live in may result from the subtle, and not-so-subtle, expectations of the people around us. It may be the decision that the problem we observed is "none of our business," or it may be tuning in to the messages that support our viewpoint, while tuning out those that do not.

We live the repetitive rhythm of an average, everyday, mundane, normal, ordinary, and altogether routine world. In fact, our bodies and our minds crave the emotional and mental ease of living life on autopilot, and we often will go to great lengths to preserve this state.

Which is why, for many, a disappointment, disruption, or disaster becomes our call to adventure.

Instead of a beautifully engraved invitation delivered by a chorus of angels, our call may be a gut-wrenching kick in the ass provided by a cruel turn of fate. In *Deadpool*, Wade Wilson learns he has several forms of inoperable cancer. In *Wonder Woman*, Princess Diana's island home is invaded and its inhabitants attacked by outsiders.

In Chapter 1, my call to adventure was bearing witness to the dread and fear on Flounder's face as we sat together in the casino parking lot. Before that night, the hazing I experienced was tolerable at best and inconvenient at worst. But I cared for Flounder. He was one of my very best friends, and he truly had a heart of gold. I could not stand to see him suffer like that. The result was a journey I set out on to help end hazing.

EXERCISE

Who or what is calling you? Which people or groups do you connect with? Whose experience or suffering attracts your attention?

_____

_____

_____

What causes do you care about? _____

_____

_____

What challenges do you see in your organization or in your community?

_____

_____

_____

What issues, problems, or topics capture your interest? What do you talk about most frequently with family, friends, colleagues, neighbors, etc.? What themes would you find by reviewing your social media?

_____

_____

_____

What experiences, knowledge, or talents could you leverage to serve others? How could you leverage them?

_____

_____

_____

SUMMARY

Let's be clear. The call to adventure is not a call for achievement, per-fection, or even success. It is aptly named the call to adventure because it is the call to accept a challenge, embark on a journey, and discover a new way.

To accept the adventure is not to know the destination or the outcome, only the path and the process.

You can try something adventurous. Try something different. Try something new. Go beyond the average, everyday, and ordinary choices for which so many people settle. In other words, make *extra*-ordinary choices.

Above all, try.

The greatest challenge each and every one of us faces is becoming ourselves, becoming everything that is within us, and demonstrating that power with consistency through action, regardless of the fears and pressures we face. To do this, you have to look within and answer the questions: Who am I? How do I see myself in the world?

Are you ready to embark on a journey to transform the world, if even for just one person?

What if that one person is *you*?

Our cultures and our societies continue to go back, time and time again, to the well of the hero's journey for the plots of our books, our movies, and our myths, but the reason is not just because the hero's journey makes a great story. It's because it is a deep, meaningful call to fulfill our potential as human beings.

There is a hero in all of us.

CHAPTER 5

BELIEVING IN YOURSELF

"There is only one way to avoid criticism: do nothing,
say nothing, and be nothing."

— Aristotle

Do you believe there is a hero inside of *you*?

In the last chapter, we discussed the hero's journey as an instruction manual for our lives, and we listened for our own unique call to adventure.

In each of our lives, we are content doing what we have always done: living ordinary lives and stagnating in our own personal status quo. Then, all of a sudden, we are awakened to the incredible opportunities and potential that exist for our organizations, communities, world, and most of all, ourselves.

Our thoughts begin to live in the powerful and wonderful world of "What if…." Our thoughts transport our dreams and our energies to a place where we can do something to make a difference. What a better place the world would be if only….

But then a hard truth smacks us in the face, causing us to stumble back toward our own stagnation. The truth is that by accepting the challenge, by answering the call to adventure, and by embarking on the hero's journey, we are risking…well, everything.

By embarking on the hero's journey, we are choosing to let go of the certainty, reliability, and stability we know so well. We are choosing to let go of everything we know for the sake of a great big unknown.

EVERY HERO HAS A PAST

One of the biggest obstacles we face is that we often don't think we are good enough to be a hero. We think that, because of mistakes we have made in the past, we are somehow unqualified or unworthy of being a hero.

But that could not be further from the truth! As Irish playwright Oscar Wilde said, "Every saint has a past, and every sinner has a future."

From ancient myths to George Washington to you, every hero has flaws because every hero is first and foremost a human being. Often, when we look at our heroes, we lift them onto impossible pedestals, forgetting they are just like us.

For example, consider the story of Larry Lawton. In 1996, Lawton was on the FBI's most wanted list for jewelry store robberies he committed on the US East Coast. Over seven years, he robbed twenty stores, stealing more than $15 million in diamonds alone.

The allure of his own power was overwhelming for him. "You become bigger and bigger, and your power becomes more and more," Lawton said. "I don't think any amount of money would have been enough for me."

Lawton went on, "I felt like I would never get caught. I definitely thought I was better than everybody else, smarter than everybody else."

Eventually, however, he was caught. Lawton was sentenced to twelve years in prison, including an entire year in solitary confinement.

In solitary confinement, he formed a friendship with an inmate he could talk to through a vent. The friendship, though, was not meant to last.

One day, his friend confided to Lawton that he was going to kill himself. Lawton pleaded with his friend, screamed for the guards, and did everything possible to stop his friend.

But he could not stop his friend from committing suicide.

The experience brought Lawton to his knees. He then discovered it was his calling to help prevent people from ending up in that place. He established a program called "Reality Check," which works with at-risk teens, educating them on the consequences and dangers of crime.

You are the author of your own story—you can choose to be the victim of your own life, or you can choose to be the hero of your life. The choice is yours.

BACKING DOWN

Have you ever backed down? How did you feel in the immediate aftermath of that decision? Although you may have felt a certain relief in the moment, how soon did that warm feeling of safety and security give way to a cold wave of disappointment, regret, and shame?

Like many kids, one of my favorite summertime destinations was a local pool. Although a couple of other good-sized pools were close to my house, only the one about twice as far away provided the adrenaline rush my adolescent friends and I thirsted for.

The pool itself was not dramatically different from the ones closer to our neighborhood, except for one factor: it had three diving platforms, rising sixteen, twenty-four, and thirty-two feet above the water's surface. To ten-year-old me, those towers seemed to stretch hundreds of feet into the sky.

For my friends and me, there was no more credible test of one's toughness than to jump from the third and highest tower. Of course, there also was no surer proof of one's cowardice than to begin the climb to the third tower, only to slink back down—both literally and figuratively—in shame, with dozens of others bearing witness throughout the long descent.

In my own personal ascent to the third tower, I ended my quest at the first platform every single time. I was unwilling even to risk the shame of an abandoned attempt to reach and jump from the highest platform. Time and time again, I refused that particular call to adventure.

There are first and third towers that appear throughout our lives. Sometimes, we even begin the climb to that highest goal, only to turn away from our noble quest, taking the path of certainty and security.

EXERCISE

What are the third towers that you fear in your life? What goals or desires do you have for yourself, your organization, or your community?

_____

_____

_____

What are the first towers in your life? What are the destinations that offer certainty, reliability, and stability?

_____

_____

_____

In what situations do you find yourself retreating to the first towers?

_____

_____

_____

DOUBTING YOURSELF

Joseph Campbell, one of the leading mythologists the world has ever known and author of *The Hero with a Thousand Faces,* observed, "'What will they think of me?' must be put aside for bliss."

Bliss. It sounds wonderful, doesn't it?

What would you give up for bliss?

Ironically, the one thing that distances and distracts us from our bliss is often the one thing hardest for us to let go of.

"What will they think of me?"

When we focus on how others might perceive us, we not only allow those people to hold us back, but we encourage them to do so and we invite it.

As we are growing up, we look for the approval of those around us, whether family, friends, neighbors, or teachers. After all, they care for us and help us grow and develop.

However, in that process, they also are teaching us to hold ourselves back. As a parent, I have also been complicit in this training.

Last year, my wife and I decided it was time for our youngest son to learn to ride his bike without training wheels—a process never as easy as it looks on TV.

Why? A natural part of the process is falling. If our son didn't fall, he wouldn't gain the experience, knowledge, or "feel" to balance himself on two wheels. If he continued using his training wheels, those additional wheels would provide his stability. If I held onto his bike after removing the training wheels, I myself would provide that stability. The only way for him to gain the skills he needed was for me to allow him the opportunity to fall.

As a parent, I want my children to grow and develop, but I also want them to be safe and secure, and sometimes those two things are at odds. As children, we look to the people in our lives who care for us for signals of what we should or should not do, and over time, we begin looking to our friends and peers for those very same signals.

Eventually, we internalize these signals and wonder, "What will they think of me?"

If you encourage your organization to end a popular, but unproductive program in order to do something innovative, but uncertain, will the members of your organization call you daring, or foolish?

If you say something when you see people bullying, hazing, or otherwise hurting others, will they see you as a stand-up person or a stick-in-the-mud?

If you stand up and voice your concerns about fulfilling your organization's mission and values, what will others think of you?

If you want to help and serve others, will you have the leadership, patience, skills, and time to make a meaningful difference, or will you simply waste your time?

If you quit your safe and secure job to pursue your passion, will your family, friends, and neighbors support you, or will they say you're being reckless or selfish?

If you try to change the world—your world, no matter how big or small that world may be—what happens if you fail? What if you let others down? What if you let yourself down?

You will find yourself out there on the edge of your own third tower. You will be on your own.

All of us have been reluctant, or we have outright refused, to accept the power of the opportunities we have in our lives. We have doubts about the outcome, process, and timing, but most of all, we have doubts about ourselves and our own abilities. We ask: Why this? Why now? And why me?

It is all too easy to refuse, to say no, and to walk away.

We have fears that we may fail. We may fail to do enough. We may fail to do the right thing. We may fail to make a difference. We possess a very real possibility of falling on our faces.

EXERCISE

In thinking about the goals and desires you have for yourself, for your organization, or for your community ("third tower"), what doubts do you have about the goals themselves? (Why this?)

_____

_____

_____

What doubts do you have about the timing of your goals and desires? (Why now?)

_____

_____

_____

What doubts do you have about yourself and your abilities? (Why me?)

_____

_____

_____

DISPELLING YOUR DOUBTS

In 2007, I received an "Anti-Hazing Hero Award," but even then, it was difficult for me to accept the label of "hero." In fact, although I had done a lot of research and work in the area of hazing prevention, I still had not publicly shared the story of my own personal experience with hazing as a college student.

I told myself my experience with hazing was private and special to me, that telling my story would somehow cheapen or diminish it. In my mind, I was not particularly successful at addressing the hazing I experienced in my organization. In my mind, my story was more powerful for me as an ongoing personal source of motivation than it ever could be for a public audience. I thought, "Who am I to speak from the stage?"

Marianne Williamson, author, lecturer, and spiritual teacher, said, "Our deepest fear is not that we are inadequate. Our deepest fear is that we are powerful beyond measure. It is our light, not our darkness that most frightens us. We ask ourselves, 'Who am I to be brilliant, gorgeous, talented, fabulous?' Actually, who are you not to be?"

We have a hero problem in our world today. We have lifted up other human beings to a level that the rest of us cannot possibly reach. We have convinced ourselves that we are not like them, that we _cannot_ be like them. We have separated them from the rest of us and made heroism an impossible and unreachable title.

To be clear, this doesn't mean that we need to diminish the extraordinary and heroic feats accomplished by heroes in the past, but instead, it is a call to connect with their humanity so we can see ourselves in them.

To illustrate this point, let's look at the life of Dr. Martin Luther King, Jr., one of the most celebrated and oft-cited heroes in history.

In "The Banality of Heroism," Zeno Franco and Philip Zimbardo identified the critical components of heroism: A quest to preserve an ideal/value or life, confronting an actual or anticipated risk/sacrifice, and engaging actively (fighting) or passively (resisting) in either a one-time act or ongoing commitment to that quest.

Martin Luther King, Jr. was an exemplar of each and every one of those components: he demonstrated his values in order to achieve an ideal (equality for all people); he persevered through threats every day and gave his life as the ultimate sacrifice; he captivated our imaginations through his words and nonviolent resistance; and he publicly sustained this arduous work for more than twelve years.

Nonetheless, as larger-than-life as the legacy of King may seem, it is in the less public and triumphant times of his life that we can find comfort in our own struggles and the strength to act on our values. As each generation remembers the stories of its heroes, those once-mortal figures become immortal legends—their once-real doubts, fears, and humanity are eroded by the sands of time.

According to author David Garrow in *Bearing the Cross*, in 1955, as King's rising star was met with a rising tide of opposition and threats, King said, "I was ready to give up. With my cup of coffee sitting untouched before me, I tried to think of a way to move out of the picture without appearing a coward."

Then he prayed, "Lord, I'm down here trying to do what's right. I think I'm right. I think the cause that we represent is right. But Lord, I must confess that I'm weak now. I'm faltering. I'm losing my courage. And I can't let the people see me like this because if they see me weak and losing my courage, they will begin to get weak."

On the very same day he was assassinated, King felt the weight of the world. According to his closest confidants, he was discouraged, had doubts, and had trouble sleeping. In Washington, DC, his plans for a Poor People's Campaign were in shambles. A peaceful march in Memphis turned violent when some of its participants forsook King's nonviolent principles.

To be sure, none of this diminishes King's greatness—instead, it may make him the greatest teacher ever on the subject of the hero's journey.

When those of us guided by our values contemplate the historic feats of heroes such as King, we may feel discouraged or intimidated. We may stand in the vast shadows of those legends, and we may fear that we don't possess the strength to act on our ideals and make a difference.

But King may very well have agreed with us. For that reason, he may be our greatest role model and teacher, showing us the true nature of commitment, courage, and perseverance, but also the very real doubts and fears we all face in our journeys.

DISCOVERING YOUR POTENTIAL

Hundreds of years ago, a nearly ten-foot-tall golden statue of Buddha was made in Thailand. It was eventually moved to Ayutthaya in the early fifteenth century.

One day, the people of Ayutthaya received word that one of the neighboring kingdoms was coming to attack them. The people of Ayutthaya desperately wanted to preserve the Golden Buddha, so they devised a plan to cover the statue's exterior in plaster, stucco, and bits of colored glass. In this way, the kingdom could protect the statue from being melted, plundered, or sold.

Ayutthaya was completely destroyed and the statue lay among the ruins. Despite the attack, the statue's exterior protection remained.

Over the next few hundred years, the statue was moved to various cities and temples throughout present-day Thailand and even was placed beneath a simple tin roof for twenty years.

Then in 1955, as the statue was being moved to yet another temple, during the final attempt to lift the statue from its pedestal, the supports broke, and the statue crashed hard on the ground, causing a piece of the stucco exterior to fall off. When those near the statue noticed the gold shining through, the rest of the stucco was carefully removed, revealing the very beautiful and very large Golden Buddha statue.

Each of us, like the Golden Buddha, has been covered in an exterior that obscures the true brilliance we have inside. We have gone so long without seeing that precious material inside that it can be difficult to believe it is even there.

For years, we have been told and convinced ourselves that we are nothing more than what others see.

However, we are truly capable of so much more because of what we have inside of us, if only we take the time to discover and uncover it.

EXERCISE

In the story of the Golden Buddha, the statue's true nature was visible in the beginning. Often, we can see the clues and evidence of our true potential early in our lives. What are some of the clues to your potential from early in your life?

_____

_____

_____

_____

_____

What made you different from others?

_____

_____

_____

What situations bothered you more than others?

_____

_____

_____

SUMMARY

We are our own greatest inhibitors. The biggest obstacle we face in our journeys is ourselves. We have doubts and insecurities. We crave the certainty of mediocrity. If we do not strive for success, we think we will not risk failure.

But the truth is that we must stretch to succeed. We must do the things that scare us in order not only to reveal, but fulfill the potential we have. Most of all, we must believe in ourselves.

CHAPTER 6

FINDING YOUR MENTOR

"It is our choices, Harry, that show what we truly are,
far more than our abilities."

— Albus Dumbledore

Professor Albus Percival Wulfric Brian Dumbledore, Headmaster of Hogwarts School of Witchcraft and Wizardry in the fictional Harry Potter series by J. K. Rowling, may be one of the greatest mentor figures ever written.

To be sure, he is a flawed person who has made many of his own mistakes, but in his mentorship of young wizard Harry Potter, he is careful to give Harry what he needs for his own journey, not necessarily what he wants at any given time. Dumbledore is truly playing the "long game" in preparing Harry for the young wizard's own journey.

In the previous chapter, we came face to face with every reason to be reluctant, to refuse, or to walk away. To go where nobody has gone before, we have to do what nobody has done before. In short, we give up and risk everything that has been done before and everything that we know.

It can't be worth it, right?

WHAT MAKES A GREAT MENTOR?

Out of the depths of our own doubts, fears, and uncertainties, we desperately need a nudge. We need someone who can propel us forward in our journeys, who can provoke our ability to see possibilities we had not seen before, and who can ignite within us the fire to forge ahead.

For many of us, our mentors may be family members, friends, neighbors, principals, teachers, coworkers, supervisors, coaches, teammates, or even a social media tribe. Mentors also may be aspirational, fictional, or historical figures we never actually meet. Nonetheless, whoever they may be, mentors provide a critical ingredient for the hero's journey.

In fictional stories featuring the hero's journey, mentors allow the heroes-in-training to approach their journeys with greater confidence, knowledge, insights, or training or they may even provide special tools the heroes need to succeed in their quests.

In our own journeys, the mentor role is not altogether different. So what separates the great mentors like Albus Dumbledore in literature, Obi-Wan Kenobi in film, or Oprah Winfrey in real life from everyone else? What should you look for as you seek mentors for your journey?

MENTORS SEE OUR BEST

Once dubbed the "Queen of All Media," Oprah Winfrey was born into poverty in rural Mississippi in 1954. Now she possesses an estimated net worth of $3 billion and helps others find their own immense, untapped potential. She said, "A mentor is someone who allows you to see the hope inside yourself."

Chances are that you have already benefited from mentors. For me, one of the most powerful examples was a teacher I had when I was a junior in high school, even though I did not understand it at the time.

For most of my life, I did not see myself as a leader. As I looked around at my friends and classmates, it seemed that every one of them was more of a leader than I could ever be. After all, they were constantly surrounded by groups of people and seemed to be able to influence others with ease. I, on the other hand, always felt like I was a step or two (or seventeen) behind the popular kids, forever on the outside of the "in" group.

However, Kathy Stern, who taught health and math at my high school, saw things differently. More than that, she saw *me* differently.

Near the end of my junior year, she approached me to tell me that she had nominated me for a national youth leadership conference in Washington, DC that summer.

What in the world did she see in me?

Even today, as I think back to who I was at that time, I cannot see the seeds of my own potential. I can certainly see the fruits of that potential, whether they were confronting hazing in my organization in college or looking back at my professional accomplishments or thinking about the coaching, speaking, and workshops I have done. I certainly have demonstrated leadership in my life and in my work.

But as I look back, even now, I can't see the seeds of that potential.

Our mentors see potential in us before we see it in ourselves. This may be as specific as pointing out to us our strengths or opportunities to lead, or it may be as general as a belief that each of us has unique talents that the world needs.

Whatever the case, the greatest mentors see something bigger for us than we may see for ourselves.

EXERCISE

As you look back at your life, who are some of the people who have seen the seeds of your potential? Think about family, friends, neighbors, religious leaders, teachers, etc.

_____

_____

_____

MENTORS SHOW A WAY

Benjamin Disraeli, twice prime minister of the United Kingdom and a prolific writer, believed each of us is born with immense potential. He said, "Nurture your minds with great thoughts. To believe in the heroic makes heroes."

The second clue to finding great mentors is that mentors show us there is a way. That is, they may not show us *the* way, but they show us that *a* way does in fact exist.

As we begin our journeys, sooner or later we will find ourselves "stuck" in a particular situation, and we will have no idea how to move forward toward our goal.

Some of us get stuck in the very beginning, causing us to refuse our journey, as we discussed in Chapter 5. Clearly, before we can even begin our journey, we have to have faith that a path exists to our ultimate goal.

Our mentors bridge the gap between our current situation and our desired destination, providing the spark we need for our journey.

The best part? We don't even have to know them or talk to them to get that spark.

They don't even have to be real.

Although a number of research studies have shown that reading profiles or watching movies featuring heroic figures, from Nobel Prize winners to Mother Teresa, can drive us to higher achievements in the classroom or spur a desire to serve others, recent studies by Rachel White and Stephanie Carlson have extended this phenomenon to even fictional characters such as Batman and Dora the Explorer.

As experimenters instructed the participants to pretend to be any of these powerful fictional characters, sometimes asking them to don some of those characters' props, the participants demonstrated some of those characters' best qualities and outperformed the control groups.

Believing in the heroic does, in fact, help us become heroes ourselves.

EXERCISE

Who inspires you? Who has talents that you wish you had? Who has faced the same types of challenges you are facing? Think about people you know and people you don't know. People who are living and people who have passed away. People who are real and people who are fictional. You don't have to know them to be inspired by them.

_____

_____

_____

MENTORS SHINE A LIGHT

Steven Spielberg, director, producer, and screenwriter of some of our most iconic hero stories, including *E.T.*, *Jurassic Park*, *Raiders of the Lost Ark*, and *Schindler's List*, once said, "The delicate balance of mentoring someone is not creating them in your own image, but giving them the opportunity to create themselves."

In addition to believing in us and believing in our journeys, mentors also help us see what we may not have otherwise seen.

In his book *Think and Grow Rich*, Napoleon Hill shares a true story about a prospector from Maryland during the gold rush era in the Western United States.

In that story, a man leaves his home in Maryland in search of gold in Colorado. After all, there were tales of tremendous fortunes being pulled right out of the rivers and rocks.

Soon after arriving, the man discovered what was thought to be one of the biggest goldmines in history. His dreams were coming true in a way even more spectacular than he could have ever imagined.

However, to extract that enormous volume of gold, he needed to invest in additional equipment.

So he returned home to Maryland to raise the funds he needed to buy the machinery necessary for the extensive project, taking out a number of loans in the process.

With the money raised and the machinery ready, the man returned to Colorado to dig for his destiny.

Initially, things went well. The man and his team pulled forth the first fruits of their labor, seemingly confirming that they were working one of the region's richest mines. They were well on their way to clearing their debt and collecting wealth beyond their wildest dreams.

But then the gold vein vanished. It just disappeared.

Day after day, they drilled, driving themselves deeper into debt. Each day, they dug deeper into the ground, and each day, they dug themselves deeper and deeper into a financial hole.

Eventually, the man and his team were forced to leave the mine. Trying to recoup some of their losses, they sold their equipment, machinery, and tools to a local junk man and returned home defeated and destitute.

However, back at the site of the abandoned mine, the junk man called a local mining engineer to investigate the mine before moving the machinery away from the site.

The engineer calculated that the vast vein of gold the man from Maryland had expected to find lay just three feet from the point where he and his team had given up. Just three feet!

The result, of course, was that one patient and savvy junk man made millions, just by asking for a fresh perspective. The moral: It can be easy to rely on those who are involved in the process with us and to discredit the perspectives of those who may come from a different background, who may not be on the same team as us or who may otherwise be different from us in some way.

But the ability to gain a wholly different perspective is invaluable. This is perhaps best illustrated by President Abraham Lincoln, who selected his greatest rivals to serve as members of his presidential cabinet, and went on to become one of the most admired presidents in history.

For us, mentors are able to identify and point out the "gold veins" all around us. They see the places to "dig" before we do.

Unlike the story above, however, the greatest mentors recognize that the discovery is most valuable when we find that treasure for ourselves. So rather than digging for us, or even telling us what we will find there, those mentors point us to our most promising places to start.

EXERCISE

Who can you call on to give you a different perspective? Consider people who are not the same age as you, who come from different backgrounds, who have different areas of interest, or who simply have a different perspective on a problem you're facing.

_____

_____

_____

MENTORS ARE ALL AROUND YOU

We often think of mentors as all-knowing and infallible teachers, but the truth is they can be anyone who invests in our growth and development.

Mentors do not have to have all of the answers. They only have to believe in our potential (to "see our best"), to believe in our ability to fulfill that potential (to "show a way"), and to believe that they can help us in fulfilling that potential (to "shine a light").

One of the most consistent (and indeed, persistent) mentors in my life is Chris Wegener.

I first met Chris when I was a freshman going through the fraternity rush process. At the time, he was a junior and one of the recruitment chairmen for Theta Chi Fraternity. On that very first day, Chris and I formed a fast friendship, which had me cracking jokes at his expense only a couple of hours after our initial introduction.

Later that night, I agreed to join Theta Chi, and Chris became my formal mentor as a new member of the fraternity.

Throughout my first semester in college, Chris consistently encouraged me to pursue leadership opportunities on campus. He did what probably thousands of fraternity big brothers do each and every year, not to mention countless of others who serve as mentors through various organizations.

But, at the end of that semester, the Theta Chi chapter on my campus closed its doors, not for disciplinary reasons, but for failing to pay its bills, and I decided to leave to pursue membership in a second fraternity.

Chris could have walked away without any blame or guilt, but instead, his mentorship rose to a whole new level.

Despite my decision to leave, Chris continued to invest in me, from coaching me to confront the culture of hazing in the second fraternity to pointing out a career path in counseling, higher education, and leadership development that I had not considered.

Neither of us could have foreseen the experience that lay ahead of me in that second fraternity or where it would lead me, but Chris continued to see my potential, to show that a positive way forward was possible, and to shine a light on the opportunities for me to start.

The mentoring Chris invested in me also has led me to other mentors in my life, such as Kim Novak, one of the world's leading hazing prevention educators and speakers. After conducting his own research on hazing using Kim's methodology, Chris connected me with her, and she has become one of my friends and mentors.

Today, Chris continues to be one of the first people I reach out to whenever I have a question or hit an obstacle, whether I stumble as a father or a son, a professional or a person. I don't count on him simply to give me an answer, but to help me find the answer for myself.

Despite Chris' example, our available mentors are not limited only to the people who are physically present in our lives. In fact, some of my favorite mentors have come from the bound pages on my bookshelves.

If that last sentence didn't reveal it, let's just say that I'm a bit of a book nerd. In fact, one of my wife's and my favorite date night destinations is one of our local bookstores, and it's not uncommon for us to leave with a few new additions to our shelves.

I'm also a bit of an introvert, which makes my newest mentor-finding mission more than a little surprising. You see, whenever I finish a book that inspires me in some way, I try to reach out to the author to share my appreciation. In my first post-college job, I worked for a publisher in the acquisitions department. One of my jobs was to find an interesting academic work or research study, then find a way to contact the author of that work, an experience which now makes it easier for me to find those authors who inspire me.

Once I contact an author, I receive a response from him or her about half of the time, and in a handful of instances, those relationships have carried on for several years.

In 2013, I reached out to Chris Lowney, author of *Heroic Leadership* and *Heroic Living*, among other titles, which focused on practical lessons to be learned from the founding and ongoing operations of the Society of Jesus, better known as the Jesuits. We exchanged a few messages, and we've spoken on the phone a couple of times.

In the last year, however, our relationship reached a new level. In 2016, I made the decision to join the Catholic Church. Although many factors contributed to that decision, one was my exposure to the Catholic Church, in general, and the Jesuits, in particular, through Lowney's books.

For that reason, I chose the founder of the Jesuits as my confirmation name, and I shared that decision with Lowney. At the same time, I mentioned I would soon visit Italy and asked him for recommendations of Jesuit sites to see.

What happened next was astounding. Lowney responded with several messages over the next few days, filled with little known tips and suggestions for our trip, securing us places on some of the rarest visits available in Vatican City.

But as spectacular as those were, my relationship with Lowney still had one more highlight in store.

In October, I found out that Lowney was coming to speak at a church in town. I immediately made arrangements to see him because we had not yet met in person.

On the day of Lowney's presentation, I was able to visit with him for several minutes both before and after his presentation, and he even asked me for feedback on different parts of his program, illustrating that mentorship is often a two-way street, allowing both parties to learn from the experience.

EXERCISE

Think big! Who are the people who inspire you? Consider people you know and people you don't. Consider authors, filmmakers, speakers, and anyone else who cares about the things you care about. If you don't know how to contact them, how could you find ways to contact them? Who could you connect with someone who may know how to find that author, filmmaker, speaker, etc.?

_____

_____

_____

SUMMARY

Your mentors are all around you—they probably have always been all around you, those special few who look for the very best for you, who demonstrate their hope for you, and who help you find and put your feet on the most advantageous path for you. In some cases, your mentors may be people who have been present in your life for a very long time, or they may be people whom you do not even know or who never even existed in real life. Whatever the case, look for people who can help you see your best, who can show you a way, and who can shine a light to inspire you in your journey. There you will find your mentors.

CHAPTER 7

TRUSTING THE PROCESS

"When I let go of what I am, I become what I might be."

— Lao Tzu

You are standing at the threshold.

At the threshold, the adventure begins.

At the threshold, you are standing between the choice to do what you've always done and the choice to forge a new path.

To make a difference, you have to do something different.

What makes the threshold different—a defining moment in the hero's journey—is that once you cross the threshold, you cannot go back. To cross the threshold is to commit yourself completely, wholly, and without limitation.

In the last chapter, we discussed the role and power of mentors and some ways to identify the very best mentors for you. In this chapter, we will commit to our journey, making the decision to deny our doubts and look past any obstacles in our way.

BURNING THE BOATS

Sun Tzu, a sixth century BCE Chinese general and the author of *The Art of War*, said, "When he has penetrated into hostile territory, but to no great distance, it is facile ground." Ninth century AD Chinese poet Tu Mu added, "When your army has crossed the border, you should burn your boats and bridges, in order to make it clear to everybody that you have no hankering after home."

Although somewhat dubious, legend says that this same strategy was used by Alexander the Great and Hernán Cortés, among others.

For a more contemporary perspective, consider what Jason Friend said in his book *ReWork*, "You need a commitment strategy, not an exit strategy."

What is the problem with having an exit strategy?

As long as you give yourself an "out," you will not give everything you have.

At one of my children's favorite local pools, there is a challenge course that extends between two plastic palm trees, with the goal to get from one side of the course to the other without falling into the water below.

To reach the other side, you have to traverse five floating spheres, two or three feet apart, with a cargo net stretching overhead.

Because the spheres are loosely tethered to the bottom of the pool, they are far from stable. It is impossible to maintain one foot on the first floating sphere as you place your other foot on the second. The only chance to complete the course is to abandon each sphere as you reach for the next one.

It is not intention, but action, that allows you to progress toward your goal.

It does not take long to find countless examples of how the failure to act has led to catastrophic tragedies. If Neville Chamberlain had acted, could we have avoided World War II? If George B. McClellan had acted, could the American Civil War have ended quickly?

On a personal level, how do you begin to account for the bitterness, disappointment, and frustration of those who have heard their own call to adventure but failed to act, whether it was a call to ask a stranger on a date, change careers, move to a new place, pursue a business opportunity, or stand up for a cause or issue they believe in?

The opposite of heroism is not evil, according to heroism advocate and educator, Matt Langdon, but apathy and inaction.

The process of becoming your best, the hero's journey, is not a two-hour seminar or even a month-long workshop. Becoming a hero is a commitment at your core, at the deepest levels of who you are. It is a commitment, not an intention, that will get you there.

NO APPLICATIONS, ONLY COMMITMENTS

A few years ago, a billboard on my route to work was advertising for the US Marine Corps. The billboard featured an intense-looking Marine and just a few words: "No applications, only commitments."

You could say the very same thing about crossing the threshold, or making the commitment, to the hero's journey.

Above all, the hero's journey is a commitment to action. It is a commitment to acting on your personal values at all times: every day, every hour, and even every minute. Even when you fall short, you commit to doing better the next time.

It also is a commitment to preparation and training. It is a commitment to strengthening your mind, heart, and soul. Your mind must see the opportunities to act and intervene. Your heart must beat with conviction and courage. Your soul must ground you in the person you yearn to be.

The process of becoming a hero is a struggle within yourself. The hero's journey is not for those looking for others' approval or adoration, or those who worry that others may think they are charlatans. Heroes are defined by their selfless sacrifices.

One of the best exemplars of this internal struggle is David Dunn, a character played by Bruce Willis in the film *Unbreakable*. Dunn is an average, ordinary man living in Philadelphia, working as a security guard for a local university, and experiencing a failing marriage.

When confronted by Elijah Price, played by Samuel L. Jackson, with the idea that he is an ordinary person capable of extraordinary action, Dunn makes excuse after excuse.

But Price insists. "It's hard for many people to believe that there are extraordinary things inside themselves, as well as others. I hope you can keep an open mind."

Dunn decides to open his mind and begins to believe. He makes a commitment to the hero's journey. He begins focusing on developing his heroic skills, from discerning opportunities for intervention to increasing his physical strength and capacity for action.

In one scene, Dunn goes to a very busy train station and places himself in the densest, most harried part of the crowd. Once there, he slowly stretches his arms out, aiming to come into contact with as many people as possible. Whenever Dunn comes in contact with someone else, he can see the crimes that person has committed.

As the passersby come into contact with him, he sees their misdeeds until he sees one that offers an opportunity to intervene. In this way, Dunn is honing and tuning his abilities in order to serve others.

In short, Dunn commits himself to his own hero's journey.

EXERCISE

What would it look like for you to hone your own abilities and talents? Where would you go? What would you do?

_____

_____

_____

THREE COMMITMENTS TO TRUSTING THE PROCESS

In Trusting the Process, there are three commitments we must make: a commitment to development, a commitment to patience, and a commitment to stepping forward. Let's look at each one in detail.

1. Commitment to Development

My commitment to development began when I decided I would confront hazing. I had the opportunity to begin that journey when I was chosen to serve as my fraternity's scholarship chairman.

Although a number of more prestigious and powerful positions existed where I could have sought to change the culture of hazing, the role of scholarship chairman was an opportunity for me to hone my talents and look for opportunities to intervene in the culture of hazing.

For five nights every week, I had the entire new member class away from the fraternity house. I was the only older member there, and I could safely share with them my position on the culture of hazing.

On one of the very first study nights, I took the entire new-member class to one of the classrooms on campus, along with two of my closest confidants in the fraternity. Once there, I held up and read the fraternity's national policy against hazing, as well as the university's policy against hazing. I told them I knew some things would happen that the fraternity's mission and values, the university's policies, and the three of us who were older members there that night did not agree with. I told them I did not know if I could stop it, but I told them I would try. I closed by telling them, "If you ever feel scared, threatened, or uncomfortable, come to our room and you will be safe."

That was my promise to them.

Yes, I certainly could have done more, and I frequently question whether I should have done more.

But when I'm being honest with myself, I know that I, too, was not ready, and those missed opportunities became a fire to fuel me in my own journey. In my case, not one person escaped the hazing activities by retreating to our room, although some of them were humiliated and even injured along the way.

Those first study nights were also my first attempts at confronting hazing. They were my first commitments to developing my leadership and finding my voice.

How will you begin? Who can you help?

EXERCISE

As I embarked on my journey to confront the culture of hazing in my organization, I noticed an opportunity to help and protect the new members of our organization.

Whom do you have an opportunity to help? Who could use your encouragement, insight, or talents? Who in your life is in need of a hero?

_____

_____

_____

2. Commitment to Patience

The second commitment we make in Trusting the Process is a commitment to patience.

On July 14, 2015, NASA's New Horizons mission arrived at its much-anticipated destination: Pluto. Since the spacecraft left our planet on January 19, 2006, it had traveled more than four-billion miles.

For eleven years, nine months, and twenty-seven days, NASA scientists painstakingly directed the spacecraft to its destination, employing a number of trajectory correction maneuvers along the way to ensure the craft met its precise destination: a distant dot in a sea of stars.

This, of course, does not even include the years of development that preceded the rocket's launch, a process that began in earnest when the project was officially selected for funding in November 2001.

Even this college graduate who once earned a C+ in Astronomy 103 is impressed by the dedication and patience on display in the New Horizons mission. In an era when the average American changes jobs every 4.6 years, a group of scientists have spent twice as long steering a $700 million spacecraft through the black emptiness of space.

In the world today, the only constant is change. At least, that's what we tell ourselves.

When we look at the truly heroic in our world, we see commitments of the highest degree. We see both the steadiness to stay with a seemingly insurmountable challenge and the willingness to give everything— even one's life—in sacrifice for the good of others.

EXERCISE

As the New Horizons spacecraft continues its flight to the outer reaches of our solar system, facing a flyby of Kuiper belt object (486958) 2014 MU_{69} in 2019, I ask you: What's your mission? To what cause would you be willing to dedicate yourself, to give your time and your energy to do something that once seemed impossible?

_____

_____

_____

3. Commitment to Stepping Forward

Do you want to have an ordinary life?

Ordinary is by the book.

Ordinary is going with the flow.

Ordinary is waiting for the right time to do something, to speak up, to stand out.

Ordinary is a choice.

Or you can choose to be extraordinary, to be heroic.

Once upon a time, the world was dominated by two powerful forces. These allies had once come together to defeat common enemies, but once the realities and threats of those great wars dissipated, the two forces locked themselves in a cold, intense war of competition and fear. Each force sought to prove it was more innovative, more powerful, and ultimately, stronger than the other. In the middle of the night, a wall was built separating the two forces. As the years went by, successive walls of increasing security and strength were built to continue to divide and separate.

After twenty-six years, the ruler of one of the powerful forces stood at the wall's gate and demanded that the other ruler tear down the wall. The sun set, yet the wall remained. A week passed, a month passed, a year passed. And yet the wall remained. Two years later, rumors began circulating that the gates in the wall would open. For the first time in decades, people could pass through the wall without restriction. Crowds gathered at the gates, but they did not know that the guards had been under order to expel, imprison, or even kill anyone who attempted to pass through the gates. One by one, ordinary people demanded to pass through without penalty and without restriction. As the demands grew louder and more numerous, the guards acquiesced, and people passed freely from one side of the wall to the other.

The point of the story is that one loud and powerful voice, not even that of former President Ronald Reagan—the Great Communicator—could bring down the Berlin Wall. The Berlin Wall came down because ordinary people chose to do something extraordinary. On November 9, 1989, they put their freedom and their lives on the line and attempted to pass through the gates, a movement that began with just one nameless person who demanded to pass through. Change was not the result of a presidential proclamation, but rather a bold action by an ordinary person.

We often identify heroes by the positions they *hold*, from father or mother to civil rights activist, from firefighter to search and rescue volunteers, but it is the positions we *take* when we stand for something meaningful that make us heroes. When we stand for those things, when we stand for our values, we are heroes.

The choices we make each and every day are the positions we stand for.

The world is not changed by extraordinary people. The world is changed by ordinary people who choose not to accept the status quo. The world is changed by ordinary people who choose to do something out of the ordinary. The world is changed by ordinary people who do something extraordinary.

SUMMARY

All of us want to be good people, but our desire and our intentions are not enough. In 2012, Bronnie Ware published *The Top Five Regrets of the Dying*, in which she recorded the most common regrets that her dying patients shared with her as their nurse. The most common of all? "I wish I'd had the courage to live a life true to myself, not the life others expected of me."

In other words, the most powerful regret most people have is that they did not cross the threshold, choosing to live a life of comfort and ease, rather than a life of purpose and peace.

You cannot live an extraordinary life by making ordinary choices.

PART III
APPLYING THE HEROIC ARTS

"In the habits and motions of every moment of every day of every year, whether conscious of it or not, you are practicing and honing something. You are acting and forming habits. You are creating your character. Creating your destiny. A hero acts with purpose in those actions and habits. A hero acts as the master and creator of their destiny."

— Rudy Reyes

CHAPTER 8

PASSING YOUR TESTS

"Life's a forge—Yes, and hammer and anvil, too. You'll be roasted, smelted, and pounded, and you'll scarce know what's happening to you. But stand proudly to it. Metal's worthless till it is shaped and tempered. More labor than luck. Face the pounding, don't fear the proving; and you'll stand well against any hammer and anvil."

— Lloyd Alexander

You said "yes" to the adventure, and now your initiation begins.

In the last chapter, you stood on the threshold, at the line between what is known, what is safe, and what others expect from you. In standing at the threshold, you examined all of the reasons so many people choose to embrace the status quo, to stay put, to say "no" to the adventure. You weighed those all-too-common excuses against the potential you feel inside of you—the power to make a difference for yourself and others. You yearned for more from your life.

Your heart burns with the desire to do something beyond the limits you or others have imposed. You have made a commitment to the journey, and the journey will develop and strengthen you.

And now there's no looking back.

But first, you have to pass the tests.

NOT TO BREAK YOU, BUT TO MAKE YOU

At the threshold, our challenges are internal ones. Those challenges reflect our own doubts and insecurities, from whether we are "enough" or the "right" person for this task, to whether the quest is "right" or whether the time is "right."

In crossing the threshold, we begin facing a series of tests reflecting the critical skills all heroes need.

In school, the tests we take are measures of our abilities, and we either pass or fail them. Those tests become a gateway through which we can pass or be turned away.

When have you failed a test? If we're being honest with ourselves, many of us, if not all of us, have failed many tests, from formal tests in school, to performance tests for completing particular tasks, or social tests where we must choose what is right despite groupthink or peer pressure.

For many people, public speaking is a particularly terror-inducing test, and my own experience with it was exactly that.

Although I had participated in choir and drama in grade school and high school, I was never really comfortable on the stage, particularly by myself, or when I was being myself, and not just part of a larger group. The spotlight terrified me.

By the time I was a college sophomore, I could no longer escape the inevitable. It was time for me to take a public speaking course.

The course was filled with a number of small group activities and techniques to practice, but the majority of our grade came down to drafting and delivering a speech in front of the whole class of about thirty students.

When it was my turn, I grabbed the paper on which I wrote my speech and made my way to the front of the room, feeling the stares and judgment of my peers—strangers I never interacted with again.

With that context in mind, I should have had no reason to worry about what they thought of me, but I could not escape the fear of their forthcoming scorn.

As I reached the front of the room, I could feel the pressure of the moment manifesting itself in physical symptoms. My pulse raced. My breaths became shorter, faster. My cheeks flushed. My ears turned red. Perspiration surfaced on my palms. In my mind's eye, I was a hyper-ventilating, sopping-wet mess.

But the real drama was yet to unfold.

I cleared my throat and began to speak. Syllable by syllable, word by word, my speech tumbled from my mouth. Aware of my own awkwardness, my hands began to shake. Now aware of my trembling hands, I began to shake even more. This diabolical feedback loop continued until the paper began shaking so much I could no longer read the words.

I had no choice but to stand there, trembling.

Mercifully, the professor put his hand on my shoulder and said, "Why don't you try again next week?"

When the next week and my next opportunity came, I was able to complete my speech. What was the secret to my success? I took the paper on which I had written my speech out of the equation. With the extra time I was given, I memorized my speech—I still held it in my hands as required, but I did not have to rely on it. I could focus on delivering the message, rather than my body's betrayals.

I did not conquer my fear of public speaking in that class, but it gave me the foundation for success. In that class, I found that practice and preparation could equip me to triumph through those tough tests.

Too often, we think that tests exist to measure our worthiness, but they exist to equip and prepare us for what lies ahead. In fact, the origin of the word "tests" is from the Latin word for "shell." Our ancestors first used tortoise shells, and later clay versions of those shells we know as "pots," to purify and strengthen metals they would use to create tools and weapons.

We too are strengthened through the tests we face. It is all too easy to experience a test, to fail, and to turn away. It is wholly different to continue testing ourselves, not to prove our worthiness, but rather to acquire and earn that worthiness. In other words, we do not naturally possess everything we need to find success on our journeys; rather, we gain what we need by persistently putting ourselves to the test.

EXERCISE

Think back to a time when you walked away from a test. It may have been an academic, intellectual, social, or some other type of test. In hindsight, what did you learn about yourself in walking away? Do you have any regrets? How has that experience continued to influence you?

_____

_____

_____

When have you triumphed through a test? What contributed to your success?

_____

_____

_____

In those examples where you found success, how did you demonstrate persistence? What did you learn about yourself as a result? How has that experience continued to influence you?

_____

_____

_____

PREPARATION IS THE PROCESS

One of the examples of how these tests prepare us for our greatest successes and triumphs comes from a TEDxBloomington talk by Nolan Harrison III. Harrison was a defensive lineman whose NFL career spanned ten years with Oakland, Pittsburgh, and Washington, DC's professional football teams, and who continues to serve through active roles with the NFL Players Association.

In his TEDx talk, Harrison describes how the "hero trials" were always present in his life and how they shaped not only his professional career, but also his personal values.

As a child, Harrison would watch his favorite heroes on TV and then sprint out of his house to recreate and reenact the stories and tests he had just seen his heroes go through. The question, "What would my favorite hero have done?" became a constant and ingrained part of who Harrison was in all areas of his life.

But there is no more poignant example than those times when that question compelled him to stand up for what's right. As a child, he was small, skinny and didn't play sports, so he was often the target of bullies. As he grew older and became taller than many of his peers, his friends began asking him to serve as their bodyguard.

Harrison never forgot what it felt like to be picked on, and he never forgot the lessons of his heroes. His empathy and values pointed the way, but the practice of standing up for himself and others provided his personal power and his training.

The opportunity to be a hero arrived when Harrison was studying one night in his school dorm. He heard a scream and quickly realized a female student was being assaulted in her own room down the hall.

Harrison ran full speed down the hallway without giving the situation or his response a second thought. In his talk, Harrison said his reaction to defend others had just become part of who he was. He intervened and was recognized as a hero.

But the funny thing is Harrison did not become a hero in that moment. He became a hero in every moment that led to that moment. He became a hero as he honed his core values. He became a hero as he practiced standing up for others. He became a hero in the less dramatic moments.

The dramatic incident just gave others the opportunity to see him for whom he already had become.

In our family room, which I refer to as the "Husker Room" because it is filled with memorabilia from my alma mater's sports team, I have a collection of framed images of my favorite football team with inspirational quotes across the bottom. One quote says, "Victory happens when a thousand hours of training meet one moment of opportunity."

The tests we face on our journey provide the preparation and training that result in victory.

EXERCISE

Think again about the moments in your life when you have been put to the test. How have those moments prepared you for bigger challenges? Have you already succeeded in larger challenges as a result of earlier tests? How can you draw from those experiences to strengthen and train you for future challenges?

_____

_____

_____

Nolan Harrison III carried with himself the question, "What would my favorite hero have done?"

Some of us may carry physical reminders as symbols of what we aspire to or value in our lives. For me, I have two tattoos, each of which serves as a reminder of not only one of my core values, but also a time when I held firm to those values. One, on my right ankle, is a reminder of a time when I benefitted from the courage of others who intervened to rescue me from a dangerous situation. It reminds me to pay their courage and sacrifice forward. The second, a Mayan bat glyph on my left shoulder, symbolizes rebirth and transformation. It reminds me of what is possible when we confront our fears and let go of what could have been in order to make room for what can be. These scars serve as my ongoing reminders of whom I want to be.

What symbols serve this purpose for you? They may be ideas or memories, such as they are for Harrison, or they may be physical reminders, such as things you wear or objects you display. If you don't have anything like that, how might an object or story serve as a reminder for you?

_____

_____

_____

THE HEROIC ARTS

So far in this chapter, we have discussed some examples of the preparation and training necessary to become a hero. However, there are six critical skills and tests we must pass to travel and triumph through the hero's journey. Zeno Franco and Philip Zimbardo, in "The Banality of Heroism," identified these skills and tests, which will be nicknamed here as: Question, Courage, Strength, Speed, Sacrifice, and Team. Let's look briefly at each one.

The Hero's Question: The ability to look at any situation with a discerning eye and question your role in that situation. The person who has developed this Heroic Art will challenge his or her own and others' thinking and will accept ideas only after careful examination with objective facts and his or her own guiding principles.

The Heart of Courage: The ability to connect with what is in your heart, both the things you feel (emotions) and the things you treasure (values). The person who has developed this Heroic Art will recognize how feelings such as anger, compassion, and fear affect his or her ability to act and will ground that person's decisions according to his or her beliefs, principles, and values.

The Rock of Strength: The ability to ground yourself at all times with your past, your present, and your future, to comprehend how past experiences have shaped you, to embrace all of the distinct parts of your identity, and to hold firm to the aspirations of the person you want to be, both now and in the future. The person who has developed this Heroic Art will demonstrate a strong sense of self and will not waver from that foundation despite any social or situational forces.

The Speed of One: The ability to be the first to act, despite any personal doubts or fears, or pressure from others. It is embracing one reason to act, being the first to speak up, being the first to stand out, and knowing that one can lead the way and create a movement. The person who has developed this Heroic Art will leverage the skills of Question, Courage, and Strength, acknowledge his or her discomfort, and choose to be the first to act.

The Practice of Sacrifice: The ability to offer your energy, gifts, talent, and time to something greater than yourself. It is easy to follow once someone else has shown the way, but to lead the way requires sacrifice and struggle. The greatest risk, however, is to dare to examine your everyday life, to connect with your emotions, to be your authentic self, and to step into ambiguity and discomfort to make a difference for others. The person who has developed this Heroic Art will serve others.

The Heroic Team: The ability to recruit others who will participate in the struggle with you. These others will provide valuable advice and counsel as you navigate the difficult terrain of addressing challenges, and they will provide influence or resources to smooth the struggle. In our world, we often credit a singular hero with extraordinary feats. The truth is, no hero—and none of us—does it alone. Even in the cases of heroic moments where one individual performs one individual act, that person has allies, coaches, mentors, and supporters to rely on.

The next six chapters are designed to help you develop each of the Heroic Arts.

SUMMARY

The journey to becoming the best we can be is not an easy process, but fraught with challenges and tests. The tests, however, are not there to determine our worthiness but to forge and reveal it. As when building physical muscle, we grow our personal strength the most through challenges and resistance.

Zeno Franco and Philip Zimbardo identified a set of abilities necessary for us to become heroes. The next six chapters will focus on fostering those skills. By seeking opportunities where we are challenged, we also are seeking opportunities where we can become our best selves.

CHAPTER 9

ASKING TOUGH QUESTIONS

"Don't ask whether it is going to be easy. Ask whether it is worth it."

— Michael Josephson

Are you asking enough questions? Are you asking the right questions?

In the last chapter, we discussed the tests we all face in our journey to become our best selves. Although we often associate tests with either passing or failing, these tests do not tell us whether we are worthy of the journey, but rather *make* us worthy of the journey. The tests are there to strengthen us, not discourage us.

In this chapter, we explore the first of the six Heroic Arts: The Hero's Question.

THE WRONG QUESTIONS

Sticks and stones may break my bones, but words can corrupt and change me.

That's not quite the childhood rhyme you remember, is it?

In 1947, Victor Klemperer, a commercial apprentice and journalist, published *The Language of the Third Reich*, which he compiled from contemporary notes on how the German language was twisted to serve the Nazi regime's goals and ideology.

In one of the most powerful sections of his work, he said, "No, the most powerful influence was exerted neither by individual speeches nor by articles or flyers…. Nazism permeated the flesh and blood of the people through single words, idioms, and sentence structures which were imposed on them in a million repetitions and taken on board mechanically and unconsciously."

Klemperer compared these single words, idioms, and sentence structures to small amounts of poison, which can be ingested without notice, slowly spreading before revealing their toxic nature. Klemperer's urgent plea, which was as pressing then as it is today, is to challenge and confront the language others and we ourselves use.

If we don't, it is all too easy for the poisons of division and indifference to spread.

In a final warning, Klemperer said, "At some point, the printed lie will get the better of me when it attacks from all sides and is queried by fewer and fewer around me and finally by no one at all."

The need could not be clearer or more urgent for us to ask the right questions.

THE RIGHT QUESTIONS

At the height of the Jerry Sandusky child sex abuse scandal at Pennsylvania State University in 2011, when the school's president, athletic director, and football coach were charged with failing to report suspected child abuse, obstruction of justice, and perjury, academic and non-academic leaders around the country questioned the school's handling of the scandal.

Capitalizing on this wave of criticism and indignation, Robert J. Sternberg authored an article, "What Were They Thinking?", in which he challenged the assumption that those other leaders would have done things differently. It is all too easy to be critical of others without taking a good, long look in the mirror.

In his essay, Sternberg identified three factors that inhibit our ability to address ethical challenges. They are: our own foolishness, the complexity of ethical decision making, and ethical drift. Regarding the first of these, Sternberg said, "Your biggest risk factor for foolish behavior is the belief that, while other people often act in foolish ways, you never would do so."

Aesop, a Greek fabulist and storyteller best known for *Aesop's Fables*, once told the story of two roosters vying to rule the same yard. They fought, and the loser hid in a corner of the yard. As the winner celebrated and danced, an eagle caught sight of it, swooped down, and devoured the victorious rooster. The loser ruled the yard from then on.

The moral? Pride goes before the fall.

The reasons we overlook our own likelihood to make such foolish decisions range from feelings of intellectual or moral superiority to feelings of inferiority and resignation. On one end of the spectrum, we may think we are too good or too morally strong to be corrupted by ethical temptations, or we are too powerful or smart to be ensnared by them. In a cruel twist of fate, this very attitude can lead to our downfall.

On the other side of the spectrum, we may think we have gone too far down a negative path to make a change or that we lack some necessary quality to make a successful change.

We may not even notice the problem because we are not observing and reflecting on the truth of the situation. In fact, our brains are hardwired to make it harder for us to look for contradictory evidence. This is referred to as "confirmation bias," which influences where we look for evidence and information, how we recall information and previous events, and how we make meaning of what we see.

Those of us who have accepted the call to adventure and crossed the threshold have made a commitment to develop ourselves through the tests that await us in the Heroic Arts, demonstrating not only our own humility and hunger for growth, but also that we believe it is never too late to make a change, whether in our own lives or the lives of others.

It is all too easy to tell ourselves and others to "do the right thing," but example after example through current events and human history prove the adage that doing the right thing is easier said than done.

One of the most common descriptors of this phenomenon is the "bystander effect," which entered our collective consciousness following the murder of twenty-eight-year-old Kitty Genovese in New York City in 1964.

The *New York Times* published an article a couple of weeks later describing an incredible scene of indifference, claiming that thirty-seven or thirty-eight witnesses had either seen or heard the attack on Genovese, but every one of them failed to notify the police.

The public was outraged. Psychologists were intrigued.

Psychologists John M. Darley and Bibb Latané began studying the bystander effect, which produced one of the strongest and most replicable effects in the field of social psychology.

The bystander effect is very real and includes five obstacles to action:

1. **Diffusion of responsibility:** Someone else will do something.

2. **Fear of embarrassment:** If I intervene, I'll be humiliated.

3. **Fear of retaliation:** If I intervene, the people involved may retaliate against me.

4. **Pluralistic ignorance:** Nobody else is intervening, so I'm the only one who thinks something is wrong. In other words, because nobody else is doing anything, I remain silent.

5. **Social influence:** Nobody else is intervening, so this must not be a problem. In other words, because nobody else is doing anything, I change my mind.

In addition, two other psychological factors can prevent us from acting in any given situation, and they are biases each and every one of us must contend with.

1. **Confirmation bias:** It is much easier to find information that confirms my opinion. In other words, I have to choose to look for information that contradicts my way of thinking.

2. **Survivor bias:** Because we have made it through problems in the past, we will make it through any tough situations in the future. In other words, we fail to see that our success is due to actions and choices, not just the ability to weather the proverbial storm.

Both of these biases lull us into a false sense of comfort and security, making it more difficult to challenge and question the way things are.

Sternberg offers a set of seven questions we can ask ourselves to counter the pitfalls of the bystander effect. These questions can help us identify those *serious* situations that require a response.

Situation: What is going on? Consider what's happening from every possible perspective.

Ethics: What are the ethical considerations? Remember your moral standards or personal values.

Relevance: How are you affected? Think about how you would feel, or how the people involved would feel about you, if you chose not to get involved.

Importance: Why is it necessary to respond? Think about the possible short- and long-term consequences of not responding to the situation.

Ought: What ethical rules apply? Contemplate what duty or responsibility you have in the situation.

Upstream: What consequences or outcomes are possible? Imagine and prepare for any potential negative results.

Start: How can you take a first step in responding to the situation? Act!

The goal of these seven steps is not to push us toward a "paralysis by analysis" whereby we miss the opportunity to act because we are wrapped up in questioning the situation. Instead, these seven steps can inoculate us against inaction by forcing us to consider our duties and opportunities in these types of situations.

However, one of the most common causes of paralysis by analysis is that we may see too many problems, which can make it challenging for us to discern which ones are most deserving of our attention and which are the most pressing for our community, organization, and us personally.

TOO MANY PROBLEMS

I have a test for you.

Grab your phone, tablet, or computer, and go to the homepage for your local newspaper. Or, if you prefer traditional newsprint, grab the front page of your local newspaper.

What do you see?

When I clicked on the website for my hometown newspaper, I saw titles shouting budget deficit, a sports cheating scandal, a cyberattack, natural disasters, political corruption, and traffic delays.

And those are only the ones I saw without scrolling!

Is it any wonder it can be so easy to feel overwhelmed by our world?

When we consider the critical thinking skills, the skills of the Hero's Question, which are important for discerning those opportunities for us to make a difference, we cannot forget how easy it is to be overwhelmed by the sheer number of issues we hear and read about every single day.

In addition to the more public problems we may read about, we face the challenges present in our organizations and neighborhoods. In fact, these less publicized issues may be even more relevant to us because we are forced to come face to face with them every single day.

No matter where they come from, these problems are everywhere, and they're big, complex, and scary.

But that kind of thinking will get you nowhere.

"The world you see outside of you will always be a reflection of what you have inside of you," said Cory Booker in a June 2011 speech for the *Inspire Ideas* event through Capella University. Booker, who is now the junior United States Senator from New Jersey, was at that time serving as mayor of Newark, New Jersey.

In his speech, he described his first attempt at making meaningful change in one of the roughest areas of the city.

One day, one of the long-time residents asked him to describe what he saw. When Booker began listing problem after problem, from drug abuse to rundown houses, and graffiti to violent crime, the resident responded that, as long as Booker saw only problems, he couldn't help their community.

Regardless of the circumstances around us, we have to believe in and look for hope and opportunity.

In the oft-quoted words of Indian civil rights activist Mahatma Gandhi, "Be the change that you wish to see in the world."

To be that change, we have to develop the tools of Asset-Based Thinking and focusing on the bright spots.

ASSET-BASED THINKING

According to Dr. Kathy Cramer, author of *Change the Way You See Everything*, "Asset-Based Thinking (ABT) is about knowing that future outcomes are not determined by today's realities…when you change the way you see things, the things you see change."

In other words, how can we expand the way we look at things to see not only the problems, but the opportunities, too? When we look around and see only problems, it is easy to feel overwhelmed and ask, "Where do I even start?"

But when we look around and see only opportunities, we find ourselves enthusiastically asking, "When can I start?"

BRIGHT SPOTS

The second tool is focusing on the bright spots.

In their book *Switch*, Chip and Dan Heath describe a variety of tools for leading change. One of the most provocative is focusing on the bright spots, an approach that has significantly improved nutrition in impoverished Vietnamese villages, solved behavioral and poor academic performance issues for middle schoolers, and improved performance for salespeople.

"Our rational brain has a problem focus when it needs a solution focus," say the Heaths. "If you are a manager, ask yourself, 'What is the ratio of the time you spend solving problems versus scaling successes?' We need to switch from archaeological problem solving to bright-spot evangelizing."

To focus on the bright spots, we identify the successes, large or small, and look for ways to copy, highlight, promote, and simply do more of them more often. The key questions to this approach are: 1) What is working? and 2) How can we do more of that?

UNPLUGGED

The Hero's Question is a fundamental search for truth.

One of the most famous quotes in all of cinema is Jack Nicholson heatedly stating, "You can't handle the truth," in *A Few Good Men*, but the reality is that most people really can't handle the truth. They can't handle the truth about their choices, their family and friends, or their work. They can't handle the truth about their own lives.

Few films better illustrate this idea than *The Matrix*, which also closely follows the hero's journey.

In the movie, countless human minds are plugged into an artificial reality, despite the truth that their physical bodies are little more than 120-volt batteries in green slime-filled pods. Inside the Matrix is an ordinary world, complete with everyday challenges, disappointments, expectations, and opportunities. The minds that have yet to awaken are content living an experience with no deeper meaning. They literally live out their lives with their eyes closed, seeing only what they see within their own minds. They cannot see beyond themselves.

When Neo is freed from the Matrix, Morpheus affirms that Neo is using his eyes for the first time. Open eyes are symbolic of consciousness, perception, and truth. Neo is now able, for the first time, to see both the reality of the Matrix and the truth of the world around him.

Beyond the Matrix, the world is a gritty, messy place. The challenges and threats are real, and they are severe. The choices the main characters—Morpheus, Trinity, and Neo—make are those of sacrifice, compared to the minds that continue to be plugged into the Matrix, where they enjoy elegant clothes, fine foods, and temporal pleasures.

Can you handle the truth?

Imagine an addict or alcoholic living in his own reality and denying the problems created by his obsession. The truth, delivered through a caring friend's intervention, has the power to break down psychological walls and transform the world for that one person—and maybe many others who are living in silent suffering.

Or consider an organization that chooses loyalty to the status quo over loyalty to the organization's mission and purpose. The organization's reality may be that "loose lips sink ships," but the truth is that honest conversation and commitment to purpose are the only things that will keep the ship above water. After all, a gaping hole in the ship's hull cannot be ignored, only examined and repaired, if the ship is to stay afloat.

The truth is powerful. It has the ability to save and the ability to transform.

Will you seek the truth in your community, organization, and own life?

EXERCISE

In Chapter 8, we revealed how the tests we face in life are not there to determine our worthiness, but instead to forge it, reveal it, and strengthen it. The first step is to develop and hone our ability to see situations for what they are and not take for granted our opportunities to help and serve others. But more is needed than merely seeing the problems around us. We need to select those areas in which we choose to make a difference for the people around us.

In 2008, to celebrate its ten-year anniversary, Google launched a campaign that asked for ideas to change the world. It asked the world two simple questions: What would help? And help most? Then Google asked people to consider how they would answer those two questions for eight different categories. Today, I'm asking you to consider the same two questions and categories. As you reflect and answer, consider your family and friends, your communities, your city and state, your country, and the world.

What would help? And help most?

Community: How can we help connect people, build communities, and protect unique cultures?

_____

_____

_____

Opportunity: How can we help people better provide for themselves and their families?

_____

_____

_____

Energy: How can we help move the world toward safe, clean, inexpensive energy?

_____

_____

_____

Environment: How can we help promote a cleaner and more sustainable global ecosystem?

_____

_____

_____

_____

Health: How can we help individuals lead longer, healthier lives?

_____

_____

_____

Education: How can we help more people get greater access to better education?

_____

_____

_____

_____

Shelter: How do we help ensure that everyone has a safe place to live?

_____

_____

_____

_____

Everything else: Sometimes the best ideas don't fit into any category at all.

_____

_____

_____

_____

SUMMARY

We often fail to ask questions because we are afraid of the answers or consequences that await us. We are afraid of admitting our own ignorance, so we find refuge in our arrogance. By definition, growth involves change. If we are not willing to change, challenge the status quo, and ask the tough questions, we fail to grow, we settle, and we stagnate. Seek the truth.

CHAPTER 10

EMBRACING COURAGE

"Empathy is the starting point for creating a community and taking action. It's the impetus for creating change."

— Max Carver

What does it take to act? Where can we find the push to help others?

In the last chapter, we asked the tough questions, and we searched for the truth. We answered: Who needs your help, and how can you help them? Our answers to these questions reveal not only our opportunities and our strengths, but also the first of the six Heroic Arts: the Hero's Question.

In this chapter, we will continue our exploration with the second of the Heroic Arts: The Heart of Courage.

THE CENTER OF COURAGE

What is a hero's most defining and perhaps most vital power? What is the source of a hero's greatest power? Is it herculean strength? A sharp mind? Maybe spider web-shooting fingertips? No, deeper than everything else is the hero's core.

In the movie *Iron Man*, Robert Downey, Jr.'s billionaire playboy character, Tony Stark, is attacked by terrorists, kidnapped, and seemingly mortally wounded. In the process of saving his life, a device is implanted in the middle of his chest that also provides him with extraordinary power, upon which he builds the Iron Man suit. This power is manifested in both external (the technological power of the Iron Man suit) and internal (the confidence and conviction within Stark) ways.

Pepper Potts, Stark's executive assistant and closest confidant, played by Gwyneth Paltrow, pleads with Stark to give up his hero's journey to protect his company and his personal safety. Responding to Potts' pleading, Stark says, "There is the next mission and nothing else.... I shouldn't be alive, unless it was for a reason.... I just finally know what I have to do. And I know in my heart that it's right."

Stark's physical change of heart also resulted in a metaphorical, even moral, change of heart. It gave him courage.

But what is courage?

Courage comes from the heart. It starts with integrity—being true to ourselves (knowing what is in our hearts), being authentic with others (reflecting what is in our hearts), and acting on the things that we know in our hearts are right.

Courage also derives from our compassion for others and our desire to help them. It is no coincidence that our hearts are at the biological and metaphorical centers of who we are. Our hearts are at the center of our power. Without engaging our hearts, there is no courage. Without courage, there is no power.

EMBRACING OURSELVES

Brad Childress, the much-maligned head coach of the Minnesota Vikings professional football team from 2006 to 2010, once remarked, "This Minnesota Nice thing, it's real. Minnesotans will give you directions anywhere, except to their house."

As a fourteen-year resident of a state where most people have spent their entire lives, I agree that "Minnesota Nice" is an interesting phenomenon. It implies that people are helpful, pleasant, and outgoing, as long as they aren't affected or inconvenienced at deep, personal levels.

This concept is also at the core of the "bystander effect" that we discussed in Chapter 9.

What prevents us from responding in situations where others need our help?

When we think of the word "courage," we may think of a brave knight "who would chance the perilous journey, through blistering cold and scorching desert, traveling for many days and nights, risking life and limb to reach the dragon's keep, where the brave knight would slay the dragon and rescue the princess," as the ogre Shrek reads aloud from his outhouse in the opening scene of the movie that bears his name.

A daunting feat, isn't it? Imagine yourself entering the dragon's keep, face-to-face with an enormous, fire-breathing beast, charged with defeating such a terrifying foe. After all, it's a feat that could turn many would-be heroes to toast.

In *Shrek*, the hero's sidekick, Donkey, demonstrates a different kind of courage—the courage to embrace the dragon and tame the fears that burn inside of us.

"Cor," the root of the word "courage," is the Latin word for "heart." The key to developing courage is to know what is in your heart, that is, to be honest with yourself.

Although "courage" is one of the most over-ascribed words in the world today, its original meaning was "To speak one's mind by telling all one's heart."

Today, when courage is applied as often to athletic performances as it is to heroic deeds, we have lost touch with the idea that speaking truth to power is the ultimate act of courage.

Courage is being authentic and real with yourself and with the people around you.

Heroes commit themselves to aligning their minds, hearts, and souls. In other words, we have courage when our actions and words reflect our thoughts and feelings.

If something doesn't feel right, we demonstrate our courage by giving voice to those feelings. By sharing those feelings, we compel ourselves and the people around us to reflect on the relationship of our actions, words, and values.

On the other hand, the more we hide from those feelings, or the more we shield others from our true feelings, the bigger and scarier our dragons become.

How do you not only reflect on the relationship among your actions, words, and values, but actually act on and align them with the person you want to be? Once again, the origin of the word courage shows us the way.

EMBRACING OTHERS

One of the last times my half-brother and I were together, we were laying my grandpa to rest and he was mourning the death of his cousin, who had been shot and killed while working the overnight shift at a convenience store.

Fortunately, my brother's cousin's death gave him something he needed to stop someone else's suffering.

In November 2016, the same year of our loved ones' losses and shortly after a bitterly contested presidential election, my brother and I (and over 90,000 others) were attending a football game at my alma mater, the University of Nebraska. Despite the fact that my brother is thirteen years older than me and we have different mothers, we have never been anything less than brothers.

As we walked toward the stadium on that crisp fall night, I was buzzing with excitement and looking forward to my first "home game" in several years. Entering the stadium, we passed beneath a gate with the inscription: "Through these gates pass the Greatest Fans in College Football." I'm sure many college football teams could make a comparable claim, but Nebraskans take particular pride in how they behave during games. We're knowledgeable, loyal, and passionate, but above all, we're respectful toward our team and maybe more so toward the opposing team.

In 1980, Hall of Fame football coach Bobby Bowden said, "I have been coaching college football the past twenty-eight years and have played before some great crowds in this country…. I actually had the feeling that when we upset the Nebraska team, that instead of hate and spite, the Nebraska fans thanked us for coming to Lincoln and putting on a good show…."

Once the game was underway, the atmosphere soon soured. My brother and I were in the second row up from a walkway that divided our section from the lower sections.

Seated in the last row of the section directly in front of us was a mother and three boys between the ages of six and twelve. In the row in front of us, and a few seats to the right from where my brother and I were sitting, were two extremely intoxicated men in their mid-twenties.

These two men zeroed in on the woman in front of them because of a button affixed to her backpack displaying her support for one of the two major candidates that year for President of the United States. At first, they berated her choice for president, but their abuse escalated to catcalling the mother and then yelling at her children that their mother was a bitch.

The people seated closest to the two men told them to calm down and shut up from time to time, but the respite from the two drunkards' onslaught was always short-lived.

A more permanent solution was desperately needed.

At halftime, when the two men left, you could hear our section breath a collective sigh of relief. Even as halftime ended and the second half commenced, the two men were nowhere to be seen.

Then, just as we became convinced they were gone for good, they stumbled back to their seats, even more intoxicated than before, and although their abuse was now less coherent, it was no less vitriolic.

However, before the two men returned, my brother had gone down into the concourse to get some refreshments. On the way back, he passed by one of the many police officers stationed throughout the stadium. But this police officer was not a stranger. Earlier that summer, the officer stationed in our section had been the one who responded to my brother's cousin's murder. Because my brother was the first family member to arrive at the scene, my brother knew the officer very well, and he had already alerted the officer to the trouble we were seeing in our section.

So as soon as the abuse resumed, my brother got up and slowly walked to the concourse exit to summon the police officer. The police officer then walked toward the two men and gave them a final warning.

Immediately after the police officer returned to where he was stationed, the two men bemoaned being "ratted out" and complained that fans were too touchy. Then they resumed their attacks on the mother and her sons.

This time, the police officer returned with seven other officers and escorted the men out of the stadium.

Clearly, the bystander effect was in effect. At least thirty people must have been aware of the situation, so why did few people intervene, and why did even fewer take sufficient steps to end the situation?

Unlike my brother and me, the other witnesses didn't feel empathy. Both my brother and I had experienced that type of abuse in our own lives. In addition, the children in the situation were roughly the same age as my own. In that situation, we felt our own pain from our past, and we also could see ourselves and the people we cared about in that very same spot. It was easy for us to understand what that mother and her sons were going through. Our hearts—those roots of courage—shoved us toward action in a situation where others did not see a problem worth getting involved in, were afraid of embarrassment or retaliation, or were waiting for someone else to do something.

We felt the family's pain. It resonated with us.

We couldn't sit there and do nothing. Our ability to connect with that mother and her children, our empathy for them, gave us courage. And our courage gave us the power to act.

EMBRACING OPPORTUNITIES

In which situations might you need to call upon your courage? What are the different types of courage you may need?

Although you can find any number of different types of courage with a quick Google search, one of my personal favorite lists comes from Lion's Whiskers (www.lionswhiskers.com), a website developed to help parents raise their children to have the courage to embrace the challenges they'll face throughout their lives.

Here is the list from Lion's Whiskers with a few definitions from me.

Physical courage empowers us to risk our physical selves (through discomfort, injury, pain, or even death).

Social courage involves resisting the urge to conform to others' expectations. It is being willing to stand out from the crowd.

Intellectual courage helps us engage with ideas that challenge the way we think and to risk making mistakes.

Moral courage is doing the right thing, particularly when we feel internal pressures (such as doing what's easy) or external pressures (such as opposition or shame). Moral courage reveals who we are through our actions and words.

Emotional courage is embracing the full spectrum of our emotions, both positive and negative. This emotional intelligence empowers us to be self-aware and vulnerable.

Spiritual courage reflects a willingness to ask the hard questions about our lives, about life's meaning and purpose.

EXERCISE

Have you ever read a newspaper story or seen a TV interview with someone who has performed some courageous feat? Even if the interviewees have different ages, genders, races, jobs, and so on, they almost always have one thing in common. When asked how they were able to demonstrate such courage, they say, "I did what anybody else would have done."

It is all too easy to take these feats of courage for granted, even in our own lives, but as we look back at our own lives with a discerning eye, we can see them as they truly are. Likewise, we can look at our daily lives for opportunities to demonstrate the Heart of Courage.

Physical courage: How have you risked discomfort or injury in the past to help others? In what ways could you help others by making yourself less comfortable?

_____

_____

_____

Social courage: How have you resisted the urge to conform to others' expectations in the past? In what ways could you help others by doing what others won't do and standing out from the crowd?

_____

_____

_____

Intellectual courage: How have you engaged with ideas that contradict your way of thinking in the past? In what ways could you help others by thinking differently?

_____

_____

_____

Moral courage: How have you fought against internal or external pressures to do what's right? In what ways could you help others by doing what's right, despite any internal or external pressures in your life?

_____

_____

_____

Emotional courage: How have you embraced negative emotions in the past to become more self-aware? In what ways could you help others by embracing difficult emotions?

_____

_____

_____

Spiritual courage: How have you embraced tough questions about your purpose or your role in the world? How can you help others through your life? _____

_____

_____

SUMMARY

Being courageous does not make you a hero, or even ensure you are following the hero's journey. Instead, courage is a component of heroism, and it is impossible to be a hero without embracing it.

In 2017, one of the greatest standard-bearers of courage finally graced the movie screen: Wonder Woman.

Wonder Woman was created by William Moulton Marston, a psychologist involved in the development of the polygraph, commonly known as the lie detector test. Through experiences with the polygraph, Marston became convinced that women were more honest and reliable than men. In 1941, he set out to create a superhero who could serve as "psychological propaganda for the new type of woman who should, I believe, rule the world," a new feminine archetype that featured women's strongest qualities.

Although the character's comic book pages and TV series have sometimes departed from the creator's vision, it was the combination of Wonder Woman's compassion, courage, integrity, and strength that created a hero stronger than many, if not all, of her male counterparts.

Given that our hearts are the greatest source of our courage, and therefore our potential power, it is only fitting to close this chapter with the closing words of the movie, *Wonder Woman.*

"I used to want to save the world. To end war and bring peace to mankind. But then, I glimpsed the darkness that lives within their light. I learned that inside every one of them, there will always be both…. Only love can save this world."

CHAPTER 11

FINDING YOUR STRENGTH

"Compromise where you can. Where you can't, don't. Even if everyone is telling you that something wrong is something right. Even if the whole world is telling you to move, it is your duty to plant yourself like a tree, look them in the eye, and say, 'No, you move.'"

— Sharon Carter, *Captain America: Civil War*

The quote above is a variation of an original quote by Captain America from *Amazing Spider-Man* #537, part of the Civil War comic event, which served as some of the movie's source material.

As a self-described "raging introvert," this quote has resonated with me for a long time.

For many months, the panel portraying the original quote served as the cover photo for my social media accounts. We often think of the courage it takes to act, but we forget the courage it takes to stand firm and tall. This strength is anchored deep within us.

In the last chapter, we discovered the heart of courage lies in embracing our emotions and empathizing with others. Doing so gives us the power to make a difference in the world.

Now, in this chapter, we will build our personal strength by planting ourselves like that tree Sharon Carter references and standing resolute.

This is the third of the six Heroic Arts: The Rock of Strength.

THE STRENGTH OF PAST, PRESENT, AND FUTURE

In *Heroic Leadership,* Chris Lowney compares the best leaders to a principle articulated by St. Ignatius of Loyola, founder of the Society of Jesus, whose members are known as Jesuits. That leadership principle is "living with one foot raised."

What does this mean?

If you are able, I invite you to pause reading right now to try this pose. If you have better balance than I do, you may be able to position yourself with one foot raised by anchoring your strength up through your toes and into the bottom of the foot that remains on the ground.

In our own lives, Lowney encourages us to anchor ourselves "by non-negotiable principles and values," like that foot that remains on the ground, while also readying ourselves "to respond to emerging opportunities" as if we are raising the other foot into the air.

By having both of our feet on the ground, we are inflexible and rigid. If we have both feet off the ground, we become susceptible to any forces that may wish to act on us and change our direction.

Similarly, the Rock of Strength is grounding ourselves in our past, focusing our goals in our envisioned future, and choosing to act on the possibilities in our present.

GROUNDING IN THE PAST

Johnson & Johnson, the makers of Tylenol, once faced one of the greatest threats any company can face, and they rose to the challenge of that threat by digging deep into their core values and their past.

The company's nightmare began when a Chicago news reporter called asking for a response to a Chicago medical examiner's press conference earlier that day saying that people were dying from poisoned Tylenol.

In the space of a few days, starting September 29, 1982, seven people died in the Chicago area after taking cyanide-laced capsules of Extra-Strength Tylenol, the painkiller that was far and away the drugmaker's best-selling product. More than that, it was one of the company's most trusted products.

Marketers predicted that the Tylenol brand, which accounted for 17 percent of the company's net income in 1981, would never recover from the sabotage.

But that prediction never came true.

Tylenol's market share spiked from 33 percent before the emergency to 48 percent just ninety days after Johnson & Johnson responded. Consumer trust in Tylenol increased three-fold compared to the period of time before the crisis, providing evidence of restored confidence in the brand.

What led to this remarkable comeback?

"We responded from our values," said Larry Foster, Corporate Vice President of Public Relations at Johnson & Johnson.

Those values were espoused by Robert Wood Johnson, a member of the company's founding family, in 1943, nearly forty years before this crisis. The very first sentence of the company's credo reads, "We believe our first responsibility is to the doctors, nurses and patients, to mothers and fathers and all others who use our products and services," and the company's leaders grounded themselves in those values before responding.

"Before 1982, nobody ever recalled anything," said Albert Tortorella, a managing director at Burson-Marsteller Inc., the New York public relations firm that advised Johnson & Johnson. "Companies often fiddle while Rome burns."

In demonstrating its responsibility to all the customers who used its products, Johnson & Johnson recalled every one of its products from every shelf in every store, not only in Chicago, and not only in the Midwest, but nationwide.

Not only that, the company actively discouraged people from buying or using any Tylenol products. Through these actions, Johnson & Johnson proved that it would not risk people's safety, even if it cost the company millions of dollars.

Then, in order to rebuild the trust it had lost when thousands of news stories nationwide that week had amplified fear, mistrust, and panic, Johnson & Johnson's leaders reached back to their values and invested the resources and time to revolutionize the packaging of their products, introducing a new triple safety seal packaging that included a glued box, a plastic sear over the bottle's neck, and a foil seal over its mouth.

In both the response to the crisis and the product's return to the market, the company put its long-established values first, rather than seeking to minimize the problem.

These leaders found immense strength in grounding themselves in their past.

EXERCISE

Often, the greatest lessons from our pasts come from the greatest mentors in our lives such as Robert Wood Johnson, the founder of Johnson & Johnson. Who are two or three of your greatest mentors, and what lessons did they teach you?

_____

_____

_____

Sometimes, our greatest values come to us from realizations that we do not want to be like certain people in our lives. In those situations, we learn whom we do not want to be, thereby valuing the absence or opposite of a quality we observed in someone. Who are two or three people in your life you want to distinguish yourself from by acting in a way completely different from them?

_____

_____

_____

FOCUSING ON THE FUTURE

What is the power of a vision?

In 2004, as Rhonda Byrne was enduring a period of personal trauma, she re-discovered a principle that soon after formed the foundation of a multimedia empire. In 2006, she released the film *The Secret*, which described the "Law of Attraction." At its core, the Law of Attraction is the idea that by focusing our thoughts on the positive things we want, we can make those things manifest in our lives.

"Ask, believe, receive," Byrne wrote.

I don't know whether I believe God or the Universe will bring those things into my life simply because I'm focusing positive energy on them, but I do believe that envisioning our future is powerful.

Other authors, such as Chris Guillebeau, who wrote *The Happiness of Pursuit*, have pointed out that great meaning and a profound sense of fulfillment await us in pursuing our own quests.

"It's about challenge and fulfillment, finding the perfect combination of striving and achievement that comes from reaching a big goal," Guillebeau said.

Our envisioned future holds great power for all of us by focusing our actions and intensifying our energy. When we focus on the kind of person we want to be, that envisioned future can serve as our North Star, guiding our path in every moment, every day, every month, and every year.

What makes me so sure?

I've been pursuing my vision since March 2000, when I participated in the LeaderShape Institute as a junior in college. The LeaderShape Institute is an immersive and intensive leadership development program for a group of seventy students. My group, after six days of engaging with our peers around common concerns, identifying issues in our communities we cared about, and learning about our own and others' leadership skills, prepared to return to campus by drafting our LeaderShape "vision."

Our vision was not only an imagined reality of where our leadership skills could take us, but a concrete map of that reality and the specific steps we would take throughout the next year to reach our goals.

What was my vision? What was that envisioned future that has been so compelling that I have worked toward it for so many years?

You're reading it. Although my actual vision on paper was long ago lost during my many moves from state to state and house to house, and although the specific steps I outlined have long since passed, my vision was and continues to be to end hazing.

I have followed that vision through addressing hazing in my own organization, researching hazing as a master's degree student, serving as a volunteer and on the board of directors for HazingPrevention.Org, and basically giving every presentation or writing every article I've ever been asked to write.

Now, although I could not have imagined this book when I wrote my vision all those years ago, the power of my envisioned future has brought me (and you) here.

The news about deaths and injuries from hazing that seemingly come out daily can be frustrating, for sure, but my vision has kept me moving forward. Your vision—whatever it may be—has the power to propel you forward and through.

As Guillebeau said, "It's better to be at the bottom of the ladder you want to climb than the top of one you don't."

EXERCISE

Vision statements are powerful because they are future-oriented, idealistic, positive, and visual, but most of all, they are compelling because they look beyond any real or perceived limits or obstacles.

Write your own vision statement below. What kind of person do you aspire to be? What do you want to achieve? Why is that achievement important to you? What would that achievement look like in its ideal, visionary state? (Hint: To make it even more powerful, write your statement in the present tense, as if you are working toward it at this very moment.)

_____

_____

_____

POSSIBILITIES OF THE PRESENT

American priest, Trappist monk, and prolific author Thomas Merton captured the importance of "presence" in his book *Conjectures of a Guilty Bystander*:

> In a time of drastic change one can be too preoccupied with what is ending or too obsessed with what is beginning. In either case, one loses touch with the present and with its obscure but dynamic possibilities. What really matters is openness, readiness, attention, courage to face risk. You do not

need to know precisely what is happening or exactly where it is all going. What you need is to recognize the possibilities and challenges offered by the present moment and to embrace them with courage, faith, and hope. In such an event, courage is the authentic form taken by love.

What are the possibilities and challenges offered by *your* present moment?

Consider: Is there any more "present" place than social media? It is impossible to digest everything that every person posts every day—and that's only the people in your own news feed!

For all of the faults of social media, its brilliance is in the moments of humor or insight that make their way into my daily life. One of my favorite moments of insight comes from "just-shower-thoughts," who wrote, "When people talk about traveling to the past, they worry about radically changing the present by doing something small, but barely anyone in the present really thinks that they can radically change the future by doing something small."

When we align our past selves by grounding who we are in our values, and when we leverage our future by focusing on the person we want to be, we are in the best possible position to "live with one foot raised," drawing strength from our past and our future. In that position, we are able to make the best possible choice in the present and to begin building a bridge between our current reality and our envisioned future.

Of all the things I like about social media, and Facebook, in particular, one of the very best as a parent is the "time hop" feature, which resurfaces past photos and posts on the anniversaries of when they were originally posted. As they show up in my news feed each day, it's fun to look back at those moments and reminisce or to think about how much my sons have grown and changed since that time.

However, for the Hockley family, those time hops can be filled with pain and regret.

Nicole Hockley looked back at a photo of her two sons playing outside in the snow in their backyard in England on December 3, 2010. One month after that, they moved to the United States, and a little more than two years after that, their youngest son would be killed in the mass shooting at Sandy Hook School in Newtown, Connecticut.

"Seven years ago on a snowy day in England. One month later we would move to the United States. I would do anything to be at this day again and make a different choice," Hockley said in a 2017 interview.

Can you imagine how crushing it would be to relive not only the shooting, but also the decision to move to the United States, over and over again? One certainly could understand why a parent in that situation may want to cling to the past, preferring to remember her child and to hold onto those memories as tightly as possible. But that would be dismissive of the possibilities of Hockley's present, not only for her and her family, but for communities throughout the country.

"The more I learned about the shooting at Sandy Hook School, the more I came to realize that it was preventable," Hockley said. "It is for this reason that the organization I helped launch and lead, Sandy Hook Promise, focuses on identifying, intervening, and getting help for individuals at-risk of hurting themselves or others."

During a speech Hockley gave at a middle school in Texas, she was asked whether she would trade all of the work she has done and all of the lives she has saved to be able to go back and save her own son. Can you imagine how gut-wrenching that question must have been for her?

Her response?

"Of course I would go back and save my son. I'm sorry if that sounds selfish, but I would do anything to have him back and for that day to have never happened. But I can't go back. None of us can. Instead, we can go forward."

The beautiful part of the present moment is that it is the only moment we have. We cannot change the past, and the future is never guaranteed to any of us. The only time we have is right now, and in that time, the people who are living the hero's journey, the people who are mastering the Rock of Strength, are using that strength to make a difference in their lives and the lives of the people around them. They're even making a difference in the lives of people they don't even know.

EXERCISE

Consider the connection between your past and your future. Look back to your answers and notes from the previous two exercises. What would a link between those two exercises look like for you? What steps can you take right now to make a difference in your own life, and more importantly, in the lives of others?

To paraphrase Chris Guillebeau, as you stand at the bottom of your own ladder, what is at the top of that ladder, and what are the first couple of rings on that ladder?

_____

_____

_____

SUMMARY

In his book *The Cathedral Within*, Bill Shore said, "A prerequisite of building out and up is to begin by digging down deep and within." The towers of the National Cathedral in Washington, DC are ninety-eight feet above ground, but 324 feet total. More than two-thirds of their strength is "down deep and within."

The very same is true for us. For all of the emphasis on outward action, our strength is anchored deep within us in our core values, in our goals and hopes for our future, and in the realization that the present is the only time we ever have.

Conventional wisdom is that you may be dealt a particular hand in life, but how you play that hand is up to you. The choices we make in the present are informed by our pasts, and they move us closer or farther away from our goals in the future. The choice to act, or the choice not to act, is always a reflection of who we are in our past, future, and present.

Find the Rock of Strength within you.

CHAPTER 12

ACCELERATING YOUR SPEED

"Action is a great restorer and builder of confidence. Inaction is not only the result, but the cause, of fear. Perhaps the action you take will be successful; perhaps different action or adjustments will have to follow. But any action is better than no action at all."

— Norman Vincent Peale

Changing a destructive or indifferent situation is extremely challenging. In fact, it may be one of the hardest things you will ever do. It can cause you to hesitate, wait, or ignore altogether your opportunity to do just one thing differently, and that one thing may make all of the difference in the world to one person.

SLOWED MOTION

Although destructive cultures can force people to become bystanders to evil, altering just a few of the variables can bring out the inner heroes in ordinary people.

For that reason, in "The Banality of Heroism," Zeno Franco and Philip Zimbardo entreated readers to cultivate heroism in response to the evil transformations they had described and studied throughout our collective history, whether in the Stanford Prison Experiment or in the abuse that occurred in the Abu Ghraib prison.

In the public health approach to violence prevention, the pivot point is winning over bystanders from inaction to action.

In Zimbardo's Stanford Prison Experiment, the guards who were perceived positively by the prisoners never complained or intervened to stop the "bad guards." In short, they succumbed to the evil of inaction. But by failing even to attempt to intervene, they were, in fact, endorsing the behavior of the bad guards. Instead of the bystander falling victim to the evil of inaction, that is succumbing to "the bystander effect," the bystander must move from the passive response of inaction to an empowered and engaged response of action.

Look at the world around you. How many examples can you find of an accident, an assault, an injury, or an injustice that would have had a dramatically different outcome if only one person would have done something differently?

What if only one person had chosen to do one thing out of the ordinary?

In the last chapter, we discovered the Rock of Strength. By grounding who we are in our pasts, by focusing on our envisioned selves in our futures, and by seeing the possibilities in the present, we find the strength that we need to make a difference.

Now, in this chapter, we take the first three of the Heroic Arts: The Hero's Question, the Heart of Courage, and the Rock of Strength, and use them to drive our action. We now possess the power to propel ourselves into action.

This is the fourth of the six Heroic Arts: The Speed of ONE.

WHAT ARE YOU WAITING FOR?

Too often, we wait for openings and opportunities. We want to make a difference. We want to change our world, whether in our families, organizations, communities, nation, or planet.

But we wait.

However, when we wait, we delay the benefits of our action. As a result, our communities and organizations stagnate and opportunities are lost. Without action, all of us struggle and suffer. Without action, we withhold opportunities for salvation and transformation.

On top of that, the pressure builds the longer we wait. As we count the minutes, hours, and days that go by, the higher the stakes climb in our minds and the more urgent the intervention becomes.

With each instance of inaction, the molehill becomes an insurmountable mountain.

In his book *The Four Agreements*, Don Miguel Ruiz observed, "Always do your best. Your best is going to change from moment to moment; it will be different when you are healthy as opposed to sick. Under any circumstance, simply do your best, and you will avoid self-judgment, self-abuse, and regret."

The benefits of getting started are both immediate and immense.

Rosabeth Moss Kanter points them out in *Four Reasons Any Action Is Better than None*:

- Small wins build confidence.
- Small wins build progress.
- A small win now is better than a big, but uncertain, win down the road.
- Winning, small or big, is contagious and energizing.

So, what are you waiting for?

SHOW THE WAY

What does it feel like to be "number one?"

In sports, to be number one is to stand at the top of your competition, your opponents, and indeed your peers. It means you are the standard against which the highest levels of success are measured. However, for many of us in our day-to-day lives, one can be a truly lonely number.

We are reluctant to stand alone, even when that action will help and serve others and when that action is based on our own deeply held values. What makes it such a challenge for so many of us to be number one? One is a critical number for us in our extraordinary journey: It takes just one person with one reason to speak up, to stand up, and to show the way.

Being number one is all about actively seeking opportunities to make a difference, to matter, to be a game-changer. To borrow a proverb from the world of sports, winners want the ball. That is, winners want to be the one who can make a difference—in fact, *the* difference—when everything is on the line.

By being the first to speak out, by being the first to stand up, and by being the one to lead the way, we also are empowering others.

Following my LeaderShape experience described in Chapter 11, I addressed the culture of hazing in my own organization that I detailed in Chapter 1. It undoubtedly was one of the hardest things I've ever done, not to mention something that could not have been farther outside my natural skillset. Even now, as a leader, I find it much more comfortable to be what I often call a "lunch pail" leader, one who does the work behind the scenes, far away from the spotlight. But as I took on the culture of hazing in my own organization, I was abruptly thrown into the spotlight. At 11:00 p.m., on April 26, 2000, I found myself standing in front of the other members of my organization, with my plans for ending hazing now exposed.

But more than that, they all were now aware that I had made public the details of the hazing that had happened throughout my two years there.

I stood there at the podium in the chapter meeting room, where thirty to forty men whom I had called "brothers" for the previous two years, many of whom I imagined standing beside me the rest of my life, were now hurling insults at me, and some of them even threatened to hurt me.

After an hour and a half, I finally was allowed to leave the room. I moved out that night, and I have not set foot in the chapter house since. In the months that followed, I resigned my membership in that organization. However, after planning a class schedule with a few of my closest friends from the organization the previous semester, I maintained a fragile friendship with those men the following term. During our shared schedules, I learned a handful of others followed me in leaving the organization that summer.

It was my own ordeal in the chapter meeting room that revealed the true nature of the organization to them, and although they either had not been present that night or did not speak up for whatever reason, they chose to discontinue their membership, too.

I may not have been successful in changing the organization's culture, but my commitment to doing what was right in that situation showed the way for others. Whether my actions empowered them, inspired them, or simply broke the ice for them, the end result was the same: If I had not been "number one," they might not have realized that being true to the people they wanted to be was even an option. They may have continued to struggle and suffer in silence.

By going where nobody else had gone before in confronting the organization's dangerous and destructive culture, I was able to show the way.

KNOW THE WAY

One of the biggest challenges you will face in showing the way is when you don't know what to do. When you have examined the situation before you, embraced your opportunity to serve others, and envisioned the kind of person you want to be, you may not know what to do in that situation.

Fortunately, the Speed of ONE also offers an acronym for addressing the situation.

One-to-one: The first strategy you can employ in addressing a problematic situation is having a one-to-one, personal conversation with any of the people involved.

iNterrupt: The second strategy is interrupting the situation, providing an alternative or distraction in order to redirect the focus of the people involved.

External: The third and final strategy you can use is involving an external party, someone outside the immediate situation, such as an authority figure.

Even when you are not sure what to do, don't let it stop you from doing something. "The best is the enemy of the good," Voltaire wrote.

Too often, we allow our desire to do the best possible thing in any given situation to keep us from doing anything. What is most important is that we do something.

"WE'RE GOING TO DO SOMETHING"

The fourth phone call came at 9:54 a.m., following three other calls a few minutes earlier from Tom Burnett, Jr. to his wife, Deena.

Deena: Tom?

Tom: Hi. Anything new?

Deena: No.

Tom: Where are the kids?

Deena: They're fine. They're sitting at the table having breakfast. They're asking to talk to you.

Tom: Tell them I'll talk to them later.

Deena: I called your parents. They know your plane has been hijacked.

Tom: Oh…you shouldn't have worried them. How are they doing?

Deena: They're okay. Mary and Martha are with them.

Tom: Good. (a long quiet pause) We're waiting until we're over a rural area. We're going to take back the airplane.

Deena: No! Sit down, be still, be quiet, and don't draw attention to yourself! (The exact words taught to Deena in Delta Airlines Flight Attendant Training.)

Tom: Deena! If they're going to crash this plane into the ground, we're going to have to do something!

Deena: What about the authorities?

Tom: We can't wait for the authorities. I don't know what they could do anyway. It's up to us. I think we can do it.

Deena: What do you want me to do?

Tom: Pray, Deena, just pray.

Deena: (after a long pause) I love you.

Tom: Don't worry; we're going to do something.

(Tom hangs up.)

At 10:30 a.m. on September 11, 2001, thirty-six minutes after the above exchange, Flight 93 crashed in an open field next to a wooded area in Stonycreek Township, Somerset County, Pennsylvania.

Of the four planes hijacked that day, Flight 93 was the only one that did not reach the hijackers' intended target. Although all forty-four people aboard were killed, not a single person on the ground was injured on a day when three other planes were used to kill thousands of people in New York City and Washington, DC.

The difference, of course, was the decision of Tom Burnett, Jr. and his fellow passengers to "do something."

The story of their heroism became personal for me on April 6, 2016, when I was invited to the closing dinner after serving as a mentor that year for the Tom Burnett Advanced Leadership Program at the University of Minnesota.

At that dinner, I heard the story of Burnett's heroism and his legacy from his own parents and sister. After such an act of heroism, it is easy to look back on the hero's life for the seeds of that heroism, from the clues in his early childhood to the formative experiences of early adulthood.

But the most impressive part to me, in the most desperate situation imaginable, was how Burnett and his fellow passengers mobilized such a rapid response to that situation.

If you knew you had only a few minutes left in your life, what would you do?

As a husband and father, it would be easy for me to take those few precious moments on the phone to tell as many people as possible how much I love them.

What would you do?

Although the Speed of ONE—as the act itself—is the Heroic Art most identified with heroism, it is the fourth Heroic Art because it cannot happen without the foundation of the first three: The Hero's Question, the Heart of Courage, and the Rock of Strength.

In the example of Flight 93, we can see Burnett asked the right questions in the transcripts of his four phone calls to his wife. We can see how he embraced courage by thinking not only of the lives on board the plane, but also those of the hijackers' potential target. In those stories shared by his family, we can see how his response was grounded in his values and personal vision for the kind of person he wanted to be. Then, in that moment, he was able to respond quickly, when time was of the essence.

When we equip and prepare ourselves to overcome any obstacles we may face, whether those barriers are our own reluctance or they are impediments that others have placed before us, we become the first to speak up, stand up, and show the way.

This is the Speed of ONE.

EXERCISE

In order to demonstrate the Speed of ONE, we must overcome any number of obstacles. Think back to times when you acted in a problematic situation, or think back to times when you did not act. What are some of the obstacles you faced in those situations? When you consider the ways you want to serve your organization, your community, or even your nation or your world, what obstacles could you face?

_____

_____

_____

Whether those obstacles are true or merely figments of our imagination, we know that we experience them as real threats. We all will face these threats. To be the one who will quickly step in, we need to be prepared. To best prepare for those threats, we have to learn to lessen the hold these barriers have on us so we can act swiftly to redirect the situation.

What strategies could you use to overcome the obstacles you have identified? How can you increase your speed in responding to situations? In what ways could you use one or more of the One-to-one, iNterrupt, or External strategies?

_____

_____

_____

SUMMARY

"He who hesitates is lost. Swift and resolute action leads to success; self-doubt is a prelude to disaster," wrote English essayist and poet Joseph Addison in his play *Cato*.

From hockey legend Wayne Gretzky, who said, "You miss 100 percent of the shots you don't take," to civil rights legend Dr. Martin Luther King, Jr., who said, "The time is always right to do what is right," the message could not be any clearer: Act. Now.

Our preparation, our studying, and our training can take us only so far, but still far short. The doubts we hold are our greatest obstacles to action. It is easy to look at a situation and see the potential negative results but much harder to think about the long-term consequences of our *inaction*.

Without action, we are lost.

CHAPTER 13

PRACTICING SACRIFICE

"Some people believe that it is only great power that can hold evil in check. But that is not what I have found. I've found it is the small things, everyday deeds of ordinary folk that keeps the darkness at bay. Simple acts of kindness and love."

— J. R. R. Tolkien

Have no doubt: You *will* change your world.

But it won't happen right away. It *will* take time.

After studying the first four of the six Heroic Arts, you are questioning your assumptions and looking for opportunities. You are connecting with your emotions and your empathy for those around you. You are aligning your actions in the present with the values of your past and your goals for your future, and you are finding the singular reason you need to speed through any obstacles in your way.

But just as you don't go from jogging around the block to running a marathon, your journey requires your patience, practice, and training. Rest assured that you are on the right path, and every step brings you closer and closer to your goal.

This is the fifth of the six Heroic Arts: The Practice of Sacrifice.

HERO TRAINING

I'm not what you would call a "weekend warrior."

Although I go to the gym two or three times each week, I do a modest amount of exercise without working toward any particular goal. I normally spend between twenty and forty minutes first thing in the morning in the pool, depending on what my work schedule allows that day. But last week, I found myself moving closer and closer to a personal milestone. I have never swum more than three-fourths of a mile.

With a little extra time one morning, I decided to go for a mile for the first time. The swim itself wasn't much different from every other swim in my life, but as I left the pool that day, I looked up the distances for triathlons out of pure curiosity to see how my swim measured against some sort of benchmark.

To my surprise, the standard swimming distance for a triathlon is 0.93 miles—less than I had just swum.

I started thinking about training for a triathlon.

But there is one thing you should know about me. I don't run. My standard response whenever anyone mentions running anything from a 5K to a marathon is, "Were bears chasing you? Because that's the only way I understand that sentence." However, even though running even 6.2 miles may seem completely out of the realm of possibility for someone like me, it *is* possible with training.

In our world, we exalt acts of heroism as one-time, life-changing, or even world-changing events, and they often are. But we fail to realize those extra-large acts of heroism are almost always preceded by countless small acts of sacrifice, dozens of medium acts of sacrifice, and maybe even a handful of large acts of sacrifice beyond the gaze of the media and the general public.

In short, those heroes have trained for those moments.

Every time you extend a helping hand at school, at work, or in your community, you are not just helping the people around you, but you also are logging a few minutes or hours of hero training. Over time, as those small acts of sacrifice become comfortable, you can begin mixing in medium acts of sacrifice, while continuing the small acts as a part of your training. Then, as you continue building your capacity for heroism, you are readying yourself for those large or even extra-large opportunities that may come your way.

BY DOING, WE BECOME

Practice may not always make perfect, but practice does in fact make permanent.

Malcolm Gladwell, in his book *Outliers*, introduced the "10,000-hour rule," which states that deliberate, intentional practice—repetition over time—is necessary in order for our dormant talents to become dominant talents.

The chemistry and structure of our brains change over time with intentional practice. The more we practice a particular behavior, the more neural pathways will form and the more they will strengthen to make that behavior easier and more natural over time. In my graduate school classes, we referred to this process as "fake it until you make it."

In *The Power of Habit*, Charles Duhigg describes how our brains are changed by the habits we create:

> This process within our brains is a three-step loop. First, there is a cue, a trigger that tells your brain to go into automatic mode and which habit to use. Then there is the routine, which can be physical or mental or emotional. Finally, there is a reward, which helps your brain figure out if this particular loop is worth remembering for the future.

And this process, repeated over time, becomes more and more automatic. That is, a habit is formed.

But these heroic habits have even deeper roots. In her book *What Makes a Hero?*, Elizabeth Svoboda shows that our brains contain mechanisms designed to provide cognitive rewards, such as positive feelings, whenever we act in altruistic and compassionate ways.

Svoboda wrote, "All of these acts arise from the same basic motivation—enriching someone else's life at personal expense, whether small or large—so the differences between them are, in part, a matter of degree."

We become heroes by practicing heroic acts, regardless of how large or small such acts may be.

Aristotle, therefore, encourages us, "Excellence is an art won by training and habituation. We do not act rightly because we have virtue or excellence, but we rather have those because we have acted rightly. We are what we repeatedly do. Excellence, then, is not an act but a habit."

As it turns out, seemingly small habits can lead to extra-large results.

A SMALL HABIT

In 1997, Richard Rescorla, a decorated former US Army Colonel, became director of security for Morgan Stanley, where he began practicing twice annual evacuation drills for employees working on the twenty-two floors of their building, most of which were between the fifty-sixth and seventy-fourth floors.

Can you imagine the drudgery and frustration of participating in those evacuation exercises every few months—trudging down floor after floor, with the frantic work of one of the world's busiest financial services firms piling up with every minute you're descending those never-ceasing stairs?

One morning, however, after a crash into the building next door, Rescorla and his employees were instructed to stay put. With the chaos unfolding next door, there was no reason for the occupants of the building immediately to the south of the crash to do anything so drastic and time-consuming.

Rescorla, however, put his evacuation plan into action. He calmly, but firmly, sent more than 2,500 people down all of those flights of stairs, two by two, as they had practiced…against the orders he had received.

The former US Army Colonel was defying orders.

Then, a mere seventeen minutes following the instructions to stay put, a second plane struck 2 World Trade Center, the South Tower, only a couple of floors above where Morgan Stanley's offices were.

Astonishingly, only thirteen of Rescorla's people perished when the South Tower collapsed just fifty-six minutes after it had been struck by the second plane.

Despite his incredible foresight and preparation, Rescorla was among those thirteen people. Why? As you might expect, he was last seen on the building's tenth floor, heading back up the stairs to save as many people as possible.

Rescorla's son, Trevor, said, "I knew he would be the last person out, because it was his command. As long as there were people in there, he would try to get them out."

His daughter also pointed out that Rescorla had helped evacuate the tower following a bombing in 1993, and his military service featured a number of stories of how Rescorla built a habit out of helping and serving others.

"I am sure that my father's background has shaped my interest in helping people. He instilled in me a sense that there is a duty to help your fellows and the perspective that we are all only a trick of fate from being in the same position [as someone else]," Trevor said.

In his sacrifice, we can see how a lifetime of practice not only prepared

Rescorla for the highest form of heroism, but continues to influence his family, his coworkers, and quite possibly many of the people who hear his story.

A SMALL START

You may look at Rescorla's story and think you will never have the foresight or the opportunity to save so many lives. You may or may not be right. But to focus only on the magnitude of the opportunity is to miss the point.

Dag Hammarskjöld, a Swedish diplomat, economist, and author who served as the second Secretary-General of the United Nations, once said, "We are not permitted to choose the frame of our destiny. But what we put into it is ours."

Even though we may not be given a frame as large as Rescorla's, we can do great things within the frame we are given.

Let's go back to our analogy of physical training for sports. Would you expect to finish a marathon without ever lacing up your running shoes before the day of the race? Or walk into a weight room for the first time and bench press 500 pounds?

It doesn't matter where you start, only *when* you start. Find a way—big or small—to go out of your way to help people on a regular basis. Not because you know them. Not because it's your job. But because they're humans in need of some type of help. More than that, see them as humans in need of *your* help.

Nicholas D. Kristof and Sheryl WuDunn may be best known for their book and PBS series *Half the Sky*, which captivated people throughout the world with real-life demonstrations that the world's greatest unexploited economic resource is the female half of the population. The authors then make the case that emancipating and empowering women is not only the key to driving economic progress, but also the best strategy for fighting poverty.

In the two Pulitzer Prize winners' follow-up work, *A Path Appears*, they share numerous opportunities for doing seemingly small things that can make a world of difference for others, whether around the corner or around the world.

Kristof and WuDunn classify these opportunities into three categories: Donations (such as money, blood, or organs), volunteering, and advocacy. They urge us, "Don't disparage the impact of a letter, or scorn a 'drop in the bucket.' That's how buckets get filled, that's how lives are changed, and that's how opportunity is created."

Just because we can't help everyone doesn't mean that we shouldn't help anyone. Sometimes the smallest thing can do more good than you could ever imagine.

A SMALL PUSH

When I attended a rush party at the Theta Chi fraternity house in the summer of 1997, I knew it was a good fit.

I had attended rush parties for various fraternities, but none of them felt like this. Theta Chi felt like home. I felt an immediate connection with the brothers of Theta Chi. I was able to sit down and talk with them as if they were long-time friends, a feeling I didn't have with any of the other fraternities I visited.

A few of us sat on the balcony, long after the rush party had ended, and talked into the early hours of the morning. At dawn, the rush chairmen took me to one of my favorite "greasy spoon" restaurants for breakfast and invited me to join. I knew at that moment that Theta Chi would be my home, and I wasted little time in signing my invitation to join, thus pledging to join Theta Chi Fraternity.

Indeed, Theta Chi was a good fit for me, and it remained so, for the most part, throughout my first semester in college.

One night in September, however, two members broke into my room and pulled me from my bed. One of them held me down while the other beat me up, offering only that I was a freshman as a reason for their actions.

The next morning when I told Chris, my friend and mentor there at Theta Chi, what had happened, he immediately brought up the incident with the rest of the chapter.

The chapter responded immediately, asking those two members to move out of the chapter house by the end of the week, even though the chapter wasn't in a good financial position and badly needed every live-in member to meet its financial obligations.

Although the decision would prove fatal to the chapter, the chapter's members demonstrated the highest levels of character and integrity in that moment when it would have been easy to overlook the incident or to sweep it under the proverbial rug.

Those men also knew the importance of passing on to the newest members a genuine understanding of those high ideals. Before initiation, every member took part in a flag drop ceremony. During the ceremony, all thirteen of us held an edge of the fraternity's flag as a narrator read a story. As the narrator described scenarios in which brothers became busy, lost interest in, or even left the fraternity, brothers dropped their edges of the fraternity's flag, and the remaining brothers tried to pick up the slack.

One by one, as the edges around me dropped to the ground, I began feeling the gravity of the membership oath I would soon take. When the ceremony ended, I was standing alone, holding the fraternity's flag.

Then, in December, the decision was made to close the fraternity chapter. We could no longer keep pace with our bills, so we would have to close the chapter and sell the fraternity house to pay the shortfall.

Although I made the decision to leave Theta Chi to join a second fraternity the next year, I took with me the examples of living with character and integrity—especially in facing hazing—that had been shared with me, and these lessons fueled my experience confronting hazing in that second fraternity as I shared in Chapter 1.

Every avalanche starts with a single snowflake. Every mountain is made of pebbles.

For me, through the example I was shown when someone stood up and fought for me, I got the push I needed to confront hazing for the next twenty years, starting with my own organization.

You may not feel like you have the power to change your community, your country, or your world, but never underestimate the power of the push you can give others.

EXERCISE

Heroes put things on the line. For the sake of something greater than yourself, you must put your energy, time, reputation, or even safety on the line.

What do you have at risk/at stake? What do you have to give up to get what you want? What can you do that others won't?

_____

_____

_____

What are some things you might have to give up to follow your hero's journey?

_____

_____

_____

At some level, in order to make an extraordinary difference, we have to give something up—pride, reputation, concern about others' perceptions, time, energy, comfort, money, other priorities—as a trade for something we find to be more valuable.

Identify three things you could lose by pursuing your hero's journey. Consider how your family, friends, community, or others may react. To what lengths will you go to advance your cause, and how will that impact your career or personal goals? Ask yourself: What is the worst that could happen?

_____

_____

_____

Identify three small acts of sacrifice you can do this week. These small acts may be anything from helping a person with a disability, a senior citizen, or single parent carry groceries to his or her car, to helping a neighbor take care of his or her yard, to making sure a friend gets home safely.

_____

_____

_____

This month, commit yourself to at least one medium act of sacrifice. You may consider giving five to fifteen hours of your time to a charitable or humanitarian organization or another comparable commitment that is meaningful to you.

The only criteria are:
- It is a selfless act. That is, you do not have anything to gain by your sacrifice.
- It should be outside your normal routine. The goal is to stretch

yourself because by stretching ourselves, we stretch to reach our fullest potential.
- You give your time. In today's world, our time often is our most precious resource. It can be easy to donate goods or money but that is also impersonal. Please give of your time and yourself.

SUMMARY

Mary Tyler Moore, who was not only one of the most accomplished actresses of her generation, but also an outspoken advocate for a number of political and social causes, said, "Take chances, make mistakes. That's how you grow. Pain nourishes your courage. You have to fail in order to practice being brave."

In the beginning of this chapter, I compared hero training to the type of training you might do for a triathlon or other sport. If you have ever done any sort of athletic or physical training, you are intimately familiar with the clichéd phrase, "No pain, no gain." Through our willingness to push through that pain, time after time, we become stronger and more powerful. As we withstand the pain that comes with sacrifice by focusing on the good we can do for others, we are building our heroic strength—our ability to act for others in critical moments. The Practice of Sacrifice provides us with the learning and strategies we need to be heroes. Remember that the Heroic Arts are not tests to be passed or failed, but ones in which to develop the skills for success.

Unfortunately, there are no shortcuts. We cannot just *intend* to be good people, to be heroic. We must practice. Aristotle said, "Whatever we learn to do, we learn by actually doing it: men come to be builders, for instance, by building, and harp players by playing the harp. In the same way, by doing just acts, we come to be just; by doing self-controlled acts, we come to be self-controlled; and by doing brave acts, we become brave." This practice does not only build our skills, but it makes it easier for us to call upon those skills in the hardest, most desperate situations.

To become the people we want to be, we have to practice and rehearse. Through a deliberate and intentional approach to becoming and building in ourselves the person we want to be, we provide ourselves with the "muscle memory" we need not only to make a difference, but to make *the* difference when we're called upon.

CHAPTER 14

ASSEMBLING YOUR TEAM

"There was an idea..." — Nick Fury
"...to bring together a group of remarkable people..." — Dr. Stephen Strange
"...to see if we could become something more..." — Vision
"...so when they needed us, we could fight the battles..." — Thor
"...that they never could." — Natasha Romanoff

The words of these five characters form the opening words of the trailer for *Avengers: Infinity War*, but they are also a callback to the formation of the Avengers in the 2012 film that brought the team of Black Widow, Captain America, Hawkeye, the Hulk, Iron Man, Nick Fury, and Thor together for the first time.

At the time of *The Avengers* release in 2012, film critics and comic book fans alike shared some concerns about how well the movie would showcase the individual heroes and stars without sacrificing the overall story.

Now, following the success of not one, but two, Avengers films, the third and fourth installments of the Avengers franchise will bring together a cast including more than sixty characters.

The making of the two movies, it seems, will mirror the challenge the heroes will face in the two-part storyline. The characters' success on the screen and the movie's success at the box office will both depend on the ability to come together as a team.

"Together a group of remarkable people…could become something more."

Like the ensemble of heroes in the movie, we have the opportunity to be more powerful together than we ever could be by ourselves.

In the last five chapters, we discussed the first five of the six Heroic Arts. As a result, you are questioning your assumptions and looking for opportunities. You are connecting with your emotions and your empathy for those around you. You are aligning your present actions with your past values and your future goals, and you are finding the one reason you need to speed toward action. You also are deliberately engaging in the practice of giving of yourself in order to serve others.

This is the sixth and final Heroic Art: The Heroic Team.

"WE" ARE GREATER THAN "ME"

From the Avengers and the Justice League to more down-to-earth examples from the 1992 United States men's Olympic basketball team to the Apollo 11 lunar mission, and from the Beatles to SEAL Team Six, the greatest heroes achieve the greatest results through great teams.

Last year, my mother-in-law texted me for gift ideas for Christmas, and after taking a few days to reply to her message, I realized there was only one thing I really wanted to find beneath the Christmas tree that year. You see, a few months before that text, I had seen an advertisement in my social media news feed for something I just *had* to have, but I couldn't justify buying it for myself.

What was this elusive item?

A "Periodic Table of Heroic Elements" sweatshirt.

And, on Christmas Eve, this particular piece of nerdy treasure was at long last mine.

What I love most about this sweatshirt is that it features more than ninety distinct superheroes, because the challenges facing our world are far greater than any one superhero can solve. We need a collection of superheroes from countless backgrounds with countless different strengths to take on the challenges facing our world.

But more than the collection of individual talents taking on individual challenges, these superheroes often come together to take on the greatest challenges of their times.

GREAT CHALLENGES REQUIRE GREAT TEAMS

The need for heroes to come together isn't true just in the comic books and on the movie screen; we can see this in real life, too. Without a doubt, one of the greatest challenges our world has ever faced was the ideology of Nazi Germany and its systematic annihilation of millions of innocent people through the Holocaust.

Although countless individuals and organizations risked everything to save others before and during World War II, the efforts of Gilbert and Eleanor Kraus were the largest private rescue mission of the war.

In January 1939, Louis Levine, the president of the Independent Order Brith Sholom, a Jewish fraternal organization based in Philadelphia, approached the Krauses about a possible mission to save dozens of Jewish children from inside Nazi-controlled Germany.

The Jewish-American couple immediately set to work, and more importantly, they began assembling their own Heroic Team.

We can learn a lot from the Krauses about building an effective team by considering how they gathered people with a variety of backgrounds and skillsets to complement their own.

Almost immediately after committing to the mission, Eleanor met with a lawyer from the Hebrew Immigrant Aid Society for advice on the complicated legal process of completing more than fifty affidavits, and Gilbert went to Washington, DC, to meet with representatives of the United States Department of State. In meetings with the Under Secretary of State George Messersmith, it was revealed there was no guarantee of success unless the Krauses traveled to Berlin to meet with the US Consul there themselves, a turn of events that required the couple to expand their team, preparing for a different mission than the one they may have originally signed up for.

While many people desperately wanted to leave Nazi-occupied Europe for the United States, the quota system in place in the United States was extremely prohibitive. For example, the 1924 US Immigration and Nationality Act (INA) placed strict quotas on immigration based on an individual's country of birth, and immigration officials also banned individuals who were not likely to find employment following the Great Depression.

In addition to the legal and logistical challenges, the Krauses faced obstacles and challenges brought by other American Jewish rescue societies that doubted the mission's legitimacy and value, as well as its means for success.

When the time came for them to travel to Austria and Germany, the Krauses asked their friend Robert Schless to travel with them. Schless, a doctor who spoke German, would be able to screen the candidates for immigration.

Gilbert Kraus and Schless arrived in Berlin on April 14, where they thought they would find the first group of children to rescue, but the Consular Chargé d'Affaires, Raymond H. Geist, informed them there were more than 200 eligible children in Vienna. They left for the Austrian capital at once. In Vienna, Gilbert met with Consul General Leland Morris and Vice Consul Thomas Hohenthal, who referred the two men to a large number of Viennese families with children who had registered for immigration to the United States, but who were lacking sponsors in the United States or who could not pay the Nazi-imposed fines.

On May 23, the Krauses acquired the necessary number of visas and purchased fifty-three passages on the *SS President Harding*, which would bring the Krauses, Schless, and fifty children from Hamburg to New York. One child who missed the opportunity to be part of the Krauses' mission was sent with his family to a Nazi-run concentration camp three weeks after the Krauses departed, demonstrating just how small the window was for success.

Thanks to a great amount of communication, planning, and teamwork, Gilbert and Eleanor Kraus were able to change profoundly the lives of fifty children. In a plan that lasted only five months from conception to completion, the Krauses proved it was absolutely essential to have a great team to have any chance of success in such a dramatic and urgent situation.

The Krauses were able to pull together a team of legal and political experts to navigate the complicated immigration process. The couple also called on their friend Schless for his language and medical expertise and enlisted the help of people on the ground in Berlin and Vienna to identify a large group of children who most urgently needed rescuing.

When thinking through the myriad challenges the Krauses faced, it can be helpful to consider concepts from the field of industrial-organizational psychology. One of the best is Lee G. Bolman and Terrence E. Deal's *Reframing Organizations*. In their book, Bolman and Deal identify four "frames" by which change agents can analyze issues and create solutions. They are:

Structural: Roles, rules, goals, policies, technology, environment

Human Resources: Needs, skills, relationships

Political: Power, conflict, competition, organizational politics

Symbolic: Culture, meaning, metaphor, ritual, ceremony, stories, heroes

You can think of the Structural aspect of the Krauses mission as the logistical part, including securing immigration and travel documents and enlisting Schless to perform health screenings. The Human Resources aspect is demonstrated by Levine approaching the Krauses to carry out the mission, as well as the conception of the mission itself. We can see the Political element in action in the involvement of the Department of State and the efforts at discrediting the Krauses by competing organizations. Finally, Dr. Schless's knowledge of the language and the involvement of sympathetic supporters on the ground in Germany illustrate the importance of the Symbolic frame.

EXERCISE

Consider the causes or issues you most care about. What can you learn about those things by considering each of the four frames from Bolman and Deal's *Reframing Organizations*?

Structural: What are the roles and rules in the situation?

_____

_____

_____

Human Resources: What are people's needs in the situation?

_____

_____

_____

Political: How are competing interests influencing the situation?

_____

_____

_____

Symbolic: How does culture influence the situation?

_____

_____

_____

Now that you have considered those causes or issues from those four perspectives, how can you enlist others to help you in addressing those challenges or capitalizing on those opportunities?

_____

_____

_____

GREAT HEROES REQUIRE GREAT TEAMS

You may not have heard of the Krauses before, but if I were to ask you to brainstorm a list of real-life heroes, it is very likely that Dr. Martin Luther King, Jr. would be close to the top of that list.

Like most heroes, King also assembled a heroic team of his own to co-create and advance a powerful vision. Through King's team, we also can see the important roles others can play on our teams: coaches, collaborators, connectors, and champions.

Bayard Rustin, who had traveled to India in 1948 to learn techniques of nonviolent civil resistance directly from the leaders of the Gandhian movement, advised King on those strategies in planning protests and rallies. Similarly, Benjamin Mays served as president of Morehouse College while King was a student there; King was impressed by Mays' emphasis on dignity for all people, as well as the disconnect between espoused American ideals and social practices.

Rustin and Mays served in the role of *coaches* for King.

There is an iconic image of King and his *collaborators* on the balcony of the Lorraine Motel in Memphis, Tennessee, on the day before his death. The men with King—Jesse Jackson, Hosea Williams, and Ralph Abernathy—were among those most actively involved in implementing the shared vision of the Civil Rights Movement. Abernathy and King co-created the Montgomery Improvement Association, a forerunner of the Montgomery Bus Boycott, and Abernathy and King co-founded the Southern Christian Leadership Conference (SCLC). Williams organized a number of demonstrations and was arrested 125 times for his participation in those protests.

James Bevel may not be as recognizable as some of the other names listed here, but Bevel had a considerable influence on the movement in his role as *connector*. Already a civil rights leader in his own right, Bevel agreed to combine forces with King in 1962, serving as the Director of Direct Action and of Nonviolent Education of the SCLC, where he developed and directed the SCLC's greatest successes, including the 1963 Birmingham Children's Crusade and the 1965 Selma Voting Rights Movement.

In developing the children's crusade, Bevel was able to bring many newcomers into the movement. In 1965, Bevel and others brought together a number of local grassroots organizations in Selma, Alabama, to launch the Voting Rights Movement.

The final key role is that of *champions*. Harry Belafonte, an accomplished and well-known actor and singer, certainly demonstrated this role by bailing King out of jail on multiple occasions and by bankrolling the Student Nonviolent Coordinating Committee (SNCC), also drawing crowds and publicity by flying to Greenwood, Mississippi, with Sidney Poitier, to provide entertainment to the SNCC crowds. Lastly, Belafonte served as a liaison between King and President John F. Kennedy.

EXERCISE

Even the greatest heroes surround themselves with other great people. As you consider your own journey, who can you add to your heroic team from each of the following categories?

Coaches: People who provide strategic advice and tactical guidance, but may not be directly involved.

\
\
\

Collaborators: People who are actively engaged in the fight; you can count on them to stand side-by-side with you in the toughest challenges.

\
\
\

Connectors: Those who can assist you by sharing ideas, trends, or visions with others. They also help you by bringing others into your movement.

\
\
\

Champions: People who provide emotional, financial, or public support. They also may help you by connecting you to others who have more power or resources.

_____

_____

_____

_____

_____

As you are assembling your Heroic Team, it is important your members represent a broad, diverse group of people.

There are three questions to ask yourself about each person in each role:
- Does the person have the ability, influence, or power to create change?
- Does the person have valuable experience or knowledge?
- Is the person credible, respected, and trusted by you, within the community, and within the organization? If you are going to count on this person, it is important that he or she has the highest levels of integrity.

GREAT TEAMS REQUIRE GREAT GAME PLANS

As a kid growing up in the Cornhusker State, the warmer months brought flag football, while the winter months brought tackle football in the snow, which meant enduring the childhood rite of passage of choosing teams.

As a kid, I never was the biggest, fastest, or most athletic, so I was often one of the last kids picked.

In choosing teams, it was essential to consider the roles you needed people to play and then to choose your team accordingly. In the warmer months, the smaller, faster kids were picked first to maximize their speed. But when we played tackle football in the snow, the bigger kids were more highly valued because a few inches of snow neutralized the speed disparity, while the larger kids were harder to tackle.

Like choosing teams at recess, before you even begin assembling your team, you have to have a plan.

First, you have to be able to describe a compelling picture of the future, or a vision that demonstrates both the role they can play and an outcome they desire. In short, you have to have an exciting idea to encourage others to join your cause. On the flip side, you also may have to address any concerns or obstacles they may see. The goal is to help others see themselves in your vision.

The next step is to convince your team that you have a specific plan for bringing your picture of the future into reality. Outline concrete, realistic steps. If you have particularly experienced or knowledgeable people on your team, enlist them in developing the strategies and timeline.

As you bring more and more people onto your team, take the time to build relationships within the team. Not only does this create a positive experience for the individuals on the team, but it also facilitates open, honest communication, which can help your team adjust to changing circumstances and identify the best people for specific tasks.

Likewise, have clear expectations for your team and vice versa. Discuss the roles and rules for each person on the team and the *modus operandi*, or way of doing things. For example, if the team has to make changes to the plan, how are the options evaluated and selected? Always have a plan for the best- and worst-case scenarios.

The final expectation is to find someone who will sustain the vision. Because the cause or issue you chose may be a deeply embedded or thorny one, it may take time for the changes to take root, and someone (or some bodies) will have to be persistent and carry the vision forward.

EXERCISE

As you build your Heroic Team, here are some things to consider when drawing up the game plan:

Is there an imminent threat to anyone's health, safety, or wellbeing? If so, do you have a duty to report that threat? (Yes, you do.) To whom can you report that threat?

_____

_____

_____

What is your vision (a compelling, realistic picture of the future)?

_____

_____

_____

What are your strategies (doable, specific steps) for accomplishing your vision?

_____

_____

_____

Who is on your team? What are their strengths? What resources do they have?

_____

_____

_____

What expectations do you have for your team and vice versa?

_____

_____

_____

Who will sustain the vision?

_____

_____

_____

SUMMARY

John Donne, an English cleric and poet, is renowned for his quote, "No man is an island, entire of itself…."

The idea of the lone, singular hero is a myth.

Too often, we take on great, heroic challenges by ourselves, carrying the weight of their success and failure on our shoulders, and the myth of the singular hero makes that weight even heavier.

But we're not alone.

Even the strongest and most powerful superheroes have families, friends, and other ordinary people who provide critical help and support along the way. In this chapter, we observed how heroes who risked everything to save fifty Jewish children during World War II didn't do it by themselves, and we also saw how Dr. Martin Luther King, Jr., collaborated and combined forces with some of the brightest and most talented people of his era.

The greatest heroes in our world surround themselves with amazing, inspiring, and strong people, who serve as coaches, collaborators, connectors, and champions. These heroes carefully examine the causes and issues they care about, and they find others who can complement their own skills. Without those Heroic Teams, our heroes' legacies may be very different.

You don't have to do it alone. Your own Heroic Team is waiting.

PART IV
CONFRONTING THE FORCES AGAINST YOU

"Don't be afraid of your fears. They're not there to scare you.
They're there to let you know that something is worth it."

— C. Joybell C.

CHAPTER 15

ENGAGING YOUR ENEMIES

"The sad truth is that most evil is done by people who
never make up their minds to be good or evil."

— Hannah Arendt

In the last chapter, we discussed the last of the six Heroic Arts: The Heroic Team. By coming together around a common cause or purpose, we become stronger than any one of us could be on our own. The people we surround ourselves with complement our skills, empower us to take on an even greater scale or number of challenges, and provide us with a strategic advantage.

But the people we encounter in our journeys are not always there to aid and assist us. In some cases, they're there to fight and resist us.

One of my favorite illustrations is the 1960 woodcut by M. C. Escher titled *Circle Limit IV.* In the image, the viewer sees a spherical tiling of interlocking angels and demons. The message of the woodcut seems to be that the angels are defined by the demons, just as the demons are distinguished by the angels. In this contrast of good and evil, this juxtaposition of right and wrong, each of the forces finds clarity and focus.

The opposition we encounter in our lives also brings clarity and focus to the good and evil inside of us. As we discussed in Chapter 7, the choices we make are the positions we stand for, and those positions we take bring who we are into sharper view. By our choices and the positions we take, we ourselves are shown not as angels or demons, but as heroes or villains.

THE THREE Fs

For many of us, the labels of foes or villains conjure images of the biggest "bads" of books, movies, and TV, from the Joker to Professor Moriarty, or from Darth Vader to Lord Voldemort.

However, in the causes we mortals fight for, the forces that oppose us take three familiar forms: our foes, our fears, and our failures. In this chapter, we will engage our enemies, who fall into one of two types—either perpetrators or bystanders, or in other words, those who engage us by either active or passive opposition.

In whatever form it takes, the opposition we face is an anvil by which our resolve and strength are forged. The greater the strength of the opponents we face, the stronger we must become to overcome them.

FACING THE FIRE

In the history of the United States of America, few (if any) fires have smoldered for as long as our "original sin" of racism. From the slave trade to segregation, and from red lines to white hoods, racism has been woven into the very fabric of our nation.

On August 11, 2017, the crackling kindling was ignited once more.

Based on rumors that a group of so called "white nationalists" would march across the University of Virginia campus that night, a group of thirty students locked arms around the base of a statue of the third US President and the university's founder, Thomas Jefferson, thereby demonstrating a firm resolve that the unrelenting inferno of a racist ideology would not rage across their campus that night.

Around 9:00 p.m., a group of more than 250 torch-wielding, white supremacist marchers found themselves face-to-face with the small group of college students.

As the marchers began circling the statue, they hurled degrading noises and taunts at the encircled students. The verbal volleys soon escalated into physical ones, as chemical sprays and punches were exchanged. The violence and vitriol that burst through a dark and peaceful campus that night soon engulfed people throughout the world.

Less than seventeen hours thereafter, Heather Heyer lost her life and nineteen others were injured as James Alex Fields, Jr. sped his vehicle through a crowd of protestors of the white nationalist rally in Charlottesville, Virginia.

Let's take ourselves back to the group of students at the statue, who were standing up to a throng almost ten times as large as their own encircled group. Imagine yourself in that moment, staring out into the scene before you, face-to-face with hundreds of red-hot opponents, carrying torches and chanting fiercely in your direction.

Sounds intimidating, if not outright terrifying, doesn't it? There you are, fortified through the Heroic Arts and your Heroic Team, standing strong for a cause and an idea that you believe in, besieged by a countless number of your enemies.

Where do you even begin?

Fortunately, most of us do not begin in the dark of night, outnumbered ten to one. If we started there, would we have the determination and resolute spirit to withstand the heat of a moment like that? In my experience, a scene like that is the culmination, not the origination, of engaging one's enemies.

If the fights we have before us are blazing infernos, we do not begin as the elite Hotshot firefighting teams who take on the largest, most out-of-control wildfires, but at the moment when Smokey the Bear once reminded TV viewers "Only you can prevent forest fires."

In my case, it began in a second-floor bedroom of the fraternity house where I was a member at the time.

Long before I drafted my LeaderShape vision "to end hazing," I made a promise to my friend Flounder in a casino parking lot, as described in Chapter 1. Ten months after making that promise, I found myself being challenged by a small group of my classmates and pledge brothers, who disagreed with my stance that the hazing should stop.

On that night in October 1999, a group of five of us engaged in a civil, yet contentious conversation about hazing and the future of our organization, a discussion that lasted until 5:00 a.m.

The five people in the room that night included me and my roommate, both of whom were against hazing, and three others who wanted to continue the practice in our organization. For several hours, we argued the merits and miseries of hazing, citing stories to support or refute our respective sides.

At the conclusion of our meeting, one of the people who opposed my promise to end hazing, and who would become the organization's vice president the next year, paused at my doorway, turned to me, and asked, "If we continue hazing, will you report us?"

I replied, "Yes."

Visibly disappointed by my response, he turned his back and walked away.

Whether we are standing arm-in-arm taking a physical stand in public or a verbal stand in private, when we are facing active and deliberate opposition, the strength of our stand relies on our certainty, clarity, and conviction. Without that strength, we find ourselves standing on mushy, treacherous, and troubled terrain. By being bold and clear, we offer no doubt about the grounds on which we stand.

The students at the University of Virginia delivered an unmistakable message to the rallying white supremacists that said, "You will not claim this ground." In my meeting with my classmates and pledge brothers, I clearly conveyed that I would not accept the continuation of hazing in our organization; either we would end hazing on our own, or I would ask others to end it for us.

EXERCISE

Consider the causes or issues you care about most. Who might oppose you? Think about those who may oppose you because they have a different point of view, or who may lose money, power, prestige, status, etc. You also may experience opposition from those afraid of change or who fear uncertainty. You could even face family and friends who want to protect you or who don't want to see you hurt.

In the space below, list anyone who may provide active resistance to the causes or issues you chose.

_____

_____

_____

Now that you have given some thought to *who* may oppose you, how could you find a firm ground on which to stand? Remember: You don't have to find the dramatic example of standing up against hatred and racism in a public space; you can begin your fight one-to-one with the people around you.

In the space below, list in what way you can take a clear and unambiguous stand with the people you listed above. For this exercise, focus on the ground on which you'll stand, the figurative "line in the sand." Later, we will discuss how you can deliver that message and take that stand.

_____

_____

_____

ACTING AGAINST INACTION

In addition to active opposition, we also will encounter passive opposition or bystanders when we try to take action against what is wrong in our organization.

In scientific terms, Isaac Newton's first law of motion states that an object at rest remains at rest, and an object in motion stays in motion, unless acted on by an external force. If we can apply this principle to groups and organizations, you might say it is every bit as challenging to create movement against passive resistance as it is to confront and counter active resistance.

Nowhere is this more evident than in the example of Harvey Weinstein, who was sheltered for decades by a bulwark of bystanders, some of whom were willful, while others were reluctant or even ignorant of the larger system of assault, harassment, and intimidation in which they were participating, according to "Weinstein's Complicity Machine," a lengthy story appearing in *The New York Times* on December 5, 2017.

Weinstein, according to the story, was well known inside and outside his own company, not only for his sexual misconduct, but also for his vindictive and volatile nature.

In the story, reporters detailed the levers Weinstein used not only as a shield to protect himself against allegations, but also as a sword for threatening his opponents.

At the height of Weinstein's success, his studio, Miramax, boasted a large number of Academy Awards, as well as an impressive list of performers and producers. Agencies were afraid of the cost of not doing business with Miramax. *The New York Times* provided examples of media outlets being given "juicy" celebrity gossip in exchange for overlooking stories of Weinstein's offenses.

However, in other cases, people were merely ashamed of having been complicit in his wrongdoing and could not bring themselves to admit their roles in facilitating such terrible things.

"You become more and more aware of everything going on, then you re-alize what it is you're cleaning up, and you don't ever want to tell anyone that—friends, family, my parents—what kind of job this is," said Sand-eep Rehal, a former assistant to Weinstein.

The business—and its resounding success in the film industry—and the man responsible for such behavior were intertwined. Some people won-dered what would become of the company, and their careers, if Wein-stein's misconduct was made public.

Whatever the reason, the end result was the same. Weinstein's behavior continued, and more and more people suffered.

Although it is easy to focus on Weinstein, the story's villain, we cannot ig-nore the "complicity machine" that facilitated and perpetuated the story and the suffering. By practicing the Heroic Arts, found in Chapters 9-14, any of the individuals in the story could have interrupted Weinstein's ma-chine.

Whether we are going head to head with our enemies or prodding by-standers into action, we can learn a powerful strategy from some of the world's greatest architects.

BUILDING BRIDGES

Although civilizations around the world had employed arches in their designs for centuries before, the Romans are considered the masters of the technique, using arches for aqueducts, domes, doorways, and vaults. These structures are so strong that many of them, which have been standing for thousands of years, do not even need mortar to hold the stones together.

An arch requires strong and sturdy columns, but its true power is a product of its design. The semicircular design distributes compression through its entire form and diverts weight onto the supporting columns.

However, building the arch itself is the toughest part of the process because the two sides of the structure have no strength or structural integrity until they come together in the middle, where the keystone is placed. The keystone holds the two sides together.

In constructing an arch, Roman builders used a wooden frame or scaffolding on which to assemble the columns and semicircular arch, which allowed them to construct a more permanent structure. Once the more permanent structure was complete, they placed the keystone, ensuring the structure's integrity and strength for generations to come.

What can we learn from this process?

In our journeys and in every part of our lives, it is all-too-tempting to attack and fight for our beliefs and our causes from our own side, safely standing on our own column completely separate from the other side. Particularly in our increasingly fractured, partisan, and segmented world, we can see how ineffective this strategy is, both short and long term.

We have to be bridge builders.

When we do not otherwise have a way to come together, like the ancient architects, we have to offer a scaffolding upon which to build a longer-lasting, stronger union.

Admittedly, finding this scaffolding will be much easier in some situations than in others. In the tougher situations, when we cannot easily find such scaffolding, both religion and science—an oft-conflicting pair—offer the same solution:

Empathy.

Behavioral scientists have found that, when people on opposing sides of controversial issues engage in learning about the other person or find common identities with that person, such as a shared identity as a father, sister, college student, farmer, etc., they are more likely to empathize with that person and have a greater openness in considering the other person's point of view.

But, despite these findings by research scientists, one of the most insightful perspectives on this topic comes from Sean-Patrick Lovett, the Director of English Language Communications for the Vatican. I had the opportunity to meet Lovett last year when I traveled to Rome and Florence with a group of college students.

Even though Lovett primarily addressed the challenges and strengths of the de-facto multi-national corporation that many of us call the Catholic Church, it was impossible to leave that meeting without hearing a call to adventure for all of us to rise to the challenges of our disinterested and deeply divided world. Lovett said that indifference is our greatest threat. If we cannot even agree to discuss our differences, we will never solve the problems we share.

We find ourselves on the attack against those who are (or are perceived to be) against us. We identify our team and theirs, launch assault on top of assault, and pummel our opposition into submission. In the end, we find that we have not only failed to win the war, but that the costs of war are high in energy, relationships, and time.

When we experience enough of those losses, we look for the "high road," where we separate ourselves from the fray and embrace the indifference that Lovett warned against. When we withdraw ourselves, we are conceding the fight for the sake of our own ego and self-preservation.

Lovett also identified three keys to not only fighting indifference, but also to making a meaningful difference in the world: communication, compassion, and seeing ourselves as part of a larger circle in our communities and in our world.

THE CIRCLE

That every one of us is connected to every other person in the world, that we all are part of a larger circle, cannot be understated. We may dismiss the idea out of hand, labeling it as hippy nonsense, socialist rhetoric, or good old naiveté. However, any number of philosophers, politicians, and writers have invoked this idea. In fact, this profound truth can be found at the center of most, if not all, doctrines of faith. In the context of religion, consider that a common definition of sin is "separation" or "sowing division."

In the very same speech in which Dr. Martin Luther King, Jr., says, "the arc of the moral universe is long but it bends toward justice," he states, "We are all...tied in a single garment of destiny.... I can never be what I ought to be until you are what you ought to be. And you can never be what you ought to be until I am what I ought to be."

With this in mind, the circle is not only representative of the wholeness (lack of separation or "holiness") of an individual or community, but also the manifestation of strength. Our strength comes from our togetherness.

COMMUNICATION

If our circle is our foundation of strength, then communication is the scaffolding on which our relationships are built. Our courageous and vulnerable communication provides the support for trust.

It does not take very long to see the erosion of authentic communication in today's world where a large part of our discussion involves eviscerating our opponents through pre-packaged bombshells shared with us through social media. But have any of those bombshells ever changed a single person's heart? I have my doubts.

On the other hand, have I changed someone's heart as we sat at a table together? I can't speak for my influence on others, but I know some of those conversations have profoundly transformed me.

Once we possess the clarity that all of us are inextricably bound together, and the courage to engage in authentic and vulnerable communication, we gain the potential for true compassion.

COMPASSION

We often think of compassion as demonstrating charity or offering sympathy, but compassion goes beyond any fleeting emotion or momentary act. The Latin origin of the word "passion" means to endure or suffer, and the Latin origin of the word "com" means together or with.

Endure together. Suffer together.

It is through our communication and compassion, noticing that both of these contain the Latin word signifying togetherness, that the circle is complete. Whole. This togetherness, through communication, compassion, and the circle, is the keystone. Through our coming together in these ways, we can bridge the greatest differences.

EXERCISE

Who is already within your circle? Who is outside your circle?

_____

_____

_____

Now focus on the people who are outside your circle, whether they are active opponents (perpetrators) or passive opponents (bystanders), what do you think is motivating that opposition? Try to empathize with them, to put yourself in their shoes, and consider what may be driving them.

Consider who is outside your circle and why. How might you offer them the scaffolding for togetherness, engaging them through courageous and vulnerable communication?

_____

_____

_____

Continuing to consider those outside your circle, how can you empathize with them, finding opportunities to "suffer together," thereby demonstrating compassion?

_____

_____

_____

SUMMARY

By taking stands for what is right and against what is wrong, you will make enemies. Any time you create change and disrupt the status quo, you will find opposition. In some situations, those opponents may actively fight you; at other times, they may passively resist you.

Whatever form in which we find our foes, we can choose to push against them, or we can choose to work with them. The cause for which we fight is not against a group of people, but against an idea or a way of doing things. In that way, we are not sacrificing our cause, but rather welcoming more people into that cause.

Now, you are not just fighting for a cause, but you are leading a movement.

CHAPTER 16

FACING YOUR FEARS

"There is no coming to consciousness without pain. People will do anything, no matter how absurd, in order to avoid facing their own Soul. One does not become enlightened by imagining figures of light, but by making the darkness conscious."

— C.G Jung

What is your greatest fear?

What would it feel like to come face-to-face with that fear? What would you do if you were forced to confront that fear?

When I was young, my greatest fear was the basement of my house. As a kid, when I got home from daycare or school, I would start playing G.I. Joe, He-Man, or Transformers in our living room while my parents were making dinner.

Inevitably, as the imaginary battle between good and evil was reaching its crescendo in the living room, my parents would call out that they needed me to get something for their dinner preparations from the basement.

For most people over the age of ten, basements are not scary places, and I don't think our basement was much different from other houses built in the 1940s. Our basement featured cinder block walls that had been painted with a dull mustard color, the carpet was a dark brown with some orange and yellow geometric shapes, and there was some wood paneling dividing the main area from the laundry room.

Other than the 1970s style décor, there wasn't anything particularly terrifying about our basement, except the ill-positioned lighting.

So, after my parents asked me to go down to the basement to retrieve something from the freezer or a jar of canned vegetables, I would find myself at the top of the stairs, my imagination running wild.

After flipping on the light switch at the top of the stairs, I would slowly walk to the bottom of the stairs, where I was flanked on my left by one of the mustard-hued cinder block walls and on my right by a section of wood paneling. Once I arrived on the bottom step, I would pause to find the courage to dart through the darkness to the middle of the room, where a single light bulb was affixed to the ceiling, with a small chain dangling from the switch. This venture was particularly terrifying for younger me.

I took a deep breath, and then I ran for my life. At the very moment when I felt the small chain in my hand, I imagined the monsters all around me were closing in. But as soon as the incandescent bulb's glare began streaking through the room, the monsters scurried back into their hiding places.

Now comes the truly funny part of this story. After retrieving whatever item I had been sent to get, I had to turn off the light and repeat this entire process in reverse.

With the item I had retrieved safely in hand, I would hold the small chain for just a minute, summoning my courage once again. As soon as I was ready, I would rip that chain downward and take off back toward the stairs. Being only slightly more agile then than I am now, my errand would almost always end with me falling up the stairs as I ran. I can't help wondering whether my parents sent me on more than a few of those errands purely for the ensuing spectacle.

Nonetheless, as I came face-to-face with my fears in that moment, I found a way through to the other side.

In the last chapter, you confronted your foes, whether they were active opponents or passive bystanders. Whenever you do something different, you can expect an oppositional force. However, those forces are not always external ones.

Inside every one of us are two additional forces—forces that may be even more powerful than the people around us who work against us and against our cause. The first of these two forces is fear, always lurking in the dark, forgotten corners of our minds.

Now, your chance to face your fears is here.

THE CAVE

Although my basement was once a formidable foe, for many of us, dark places, from a dimly lit alley or parking lot to a dense forest at dusk, continue to produce unsettling feelings. The monsters we fear as we grow older may be uncomfortable truths we don't want to acknowledge about ourselves, our organizations, or our communities.

It can be scary even to think about those monsters lurking in the darkness, and even more terrifying to think about dragging those beasts into the light. Or maybe our monsters are our fears that keep us small, that keep us from following our bliss or living out the best versions of ourselves in the world. The longer we wait, the larger and more indomitable those monsters can become.

The secret to vanquishing monsters is to get them when they're small, before they can feed on our fears and grow in the dark recesses of our lives. The sooner we acknowledge them and deal with them, the easier we can dispense with them and become the heroes we have the potential to be.

Although the deepest fears of our childhood may have resided in our basements, closets, or attics, in the hero's journey, the place where we come face to face with our greatest fears is what Joseph Campbell referred to as The Innermost Cave.

Caves are fascinating, intriguing, and mystifying places. Even with modern equipment, to travel into the darkest depths of a cave requires great strength and resolve. In the ancient world, caves were critical components for many rites of passage. These foreboding tunnels were both passages to the underworld and the earth's womb from which initiates were reborn and transformed.

In those ancient rites, initiates departed the relative comfort and warmth of familiar worlds, entering a mysterious world shrouded by unknown and unseen challenges.

The cold, dark interior of the cave and its treacherous floors contributed physical challenges, while the deprivation of aural and visual stimuli, the dark, expansive void within, and the solitary nature of the journey provided intense psychological trials, as well.

What formidable foes await you?

Lao Tzu, a Chinese author and philosopher, wrote, "Mastering others is strength. Mastering yourself is true power."

When we embark on the experience of making a meaningful difference for our organizations, our communities, or our world, we often do so with the naive notion that only others are changing. In order to triumph through the hero's journey, you have to change as a person, letting go of part of who you are. The truth is, in order to win, you have to lose.

Your transformation is the cost of admission to the hero's journey.

"We must be willing to let go of the life we planned so as to have the life that is waiting for us," wrote Joseph Campbell, author of *The Hero with a Thousand Faces*.

Each and every time we courageously and willfully enter into situations that are difficult, stressful, or downright scary, regardless of how large or small those challenges may be, we are building our capabilities and strengths to overcome our fears in the future.

If you choose to avoid getting involved, to mind your own business, or to back down from the challenge, you are not only feeding and growing your fears, but more importantly, you are giving those fears the power to rule your life.

Our greatest potential, therefore, lies in choosing to take on our fears.

For many of us, it is easy to focus on the risks and uncertainties we see in any given situation, but the greatest reward is the confidence we gain when we push through our fears. In those moments when we are most afraid, we have nothing to lose, but we have the world to gain.

In that way, we are not helpless, passive recipients of the fears our bodies and minds force upon us. Inside all of us lies the potential not only to overcome our fears, but the power to help and serve others, regardless of how dire or foreboding the situation may be.

THE FEELING

What is fear?

Fear is a completely natural biological response we all feel many times throughout our lives. Our brain receives a stimulus, interprets it as some sort of threat, and responds by flooding our bodies with chemicals to help us deal with that situation. Our heart rate increases, our blood pressure rises, our pupils dilate, and blood begins flowing away from our brains and hearts into our extremities, engaging our muscles and preventing us from overthinking our course of action.

This response is commonly known as the "fight or flight" response.

When we encounter one of those scary things, one of our first instincts is to escape, known as the "flight" response. The adrenaline and cortisol chemicals coursing through our veins prepare our bodies for the run of a lifetime. In those moments, our fears cause us to **F**orget **E**verything **A**nd **R**un.

At other times, the instinct that pushes us is the "fight" response, in which our fears cause us to **F**ace **E**verything **A**nd **R**ise. This second response is most commonly associated with courage.

But even the seemingly brave and heroic "fight" response is grounded in self-preservation. By engaging this defense mechanism, we are only as powerful as the threat we ourselves feel in any given moment. In other words, the safer we feel, the more the chemicals that drive us in that moment will subside.

Dr. Kelly McGonigal, author of *The Upside of Stress*, has discovered that a small shift in those scary, stressful moments can tap into an even deeper reservoir of courage and heroism.

In her research, McGonigal observed a previously unacknowledged "tend-and-befriend" response to stress, which she hypothesized was an evolutionary result of our desire to protect our families and our tribes in life-threatening or stressful times.

Rather than flooding our bodies with adrenaline and cortisol, the chemicals of "fight-or-flight" and self-preservation, we can choose a different, more powerful response by focusing on protecting and serving others. When we shift our focus from self-preservation to helping and serving others, we experience a three-pronged wave of oxytocin, dopamine, and serotonin.

The combination of these three chemicals empowers us to face our fears by **F**ocusing on **E**mpathy, **A**dventure, and **R**ational thinking. Oxytocin not only helps us connect with others and empathize with them, but it turns down the volume of our brain's fear centers, making courage even more accessible to us.

The second chemical, dopamine, creates feelings of hope and also prepares our body for physical action. Together, these reactions ready us for an adventure.

Finally, serotonin enhances our perception, rational thinking, and self-control.

In short, by focusing on others rather than ourselves, we can overcome a natural physiological response of self-preservation, while gaining the compassion, courage, and critical thinking to be a hero for others in those situations.

When we focus on others rather than ourselves, our power grows, and when *the moment* arrives, we can be ready to meet it.

THE MOMENT

Do you believe in defining moments? Do you believe in moments after which things will never be the same? Do you believe in moments that divide our lives into two parts—before this moment and after? But more than all of that, do you believe in the transformative power of those moments?

I do, because I have had one of those moments.

"Dear Linda."

As the words left the mouth of the vice president of my fraternity, I knew this was one of those defining moments. After all, I was a twenty-one-year-old junior who had never been one of the popular kids. After graduating from high school with a class of thirty, I found my place among almost 25,000 students as a member of this organization. I shied away from subjecting myself to the popularity contests involved in running for the highest executive board positions in the organization, but I felt like I had found a group of men I would call my brothers for the rest of my life.

But in that moment, I knew this was one of those watershed moments when everything would change. My life would be marked before this moment and after.

"Dear Linda."

My hand rose slowly from the back corner of the room where we were meeting. The fraternity's officers had called an emergency meeting for a bogus reason to set this trap for me. They had come into possession of a couple of emails I had written to Linda, one of the university's administrators. The emails described in excruciating detail our organization's hazing practices.

When I heard the vice president say those first two words, I knew the messages he was reading from the front of the room were, in fact, the ones I had sent to Linda.

But more than that, I knew I had to own up to the words I had written, the decisions I had made, and the wheels I had set in motion. So I stood up and walked to the front of the room.

"Dear Linda," I read.

As I read from the first two words of the emails all the way through to the last of the 1,240 words I had written, disclosing the darkest, most shameful secrets of our organization, my ordeal was only beginning. The gasps of disbelief from the dozens of men in the room gave way to grumbling, which grew and grew into a less stable scene. The bogus meeting, which had begun at 11:00 p.m. on the Wednesday of finals week, ended ninety minutes later with threats of ending my membership in the organization and my life.

"So help me, I will kill you!" one person screamed at me as two others held him back.

There was before this moment, and after this moment.

Finally, mercifully, the Sergeant-at-Arms guarding the door stepped aside, and I was allowed to leave the room. The ordeal was coming to an end, but the real work was only beginning.

I believe in defining moments, not because we have to live up to our potential or to prove ourselves to anyone else. I believe in defining moments because we have to prove ourselves to ourselves. In those moments, we are transformed.

As I think back to that moment, remembering what it was like standing at the podium, defending my decisions, I know it was not me or my own self-preservation that sustained me.

If that had been the case, I know I would have been overwhelmed by fear. But more than that, if I had been overwhelmed by fear, I would have felt an immense pressure to back down. After all, I didn't have many friends at this large school, and I had even fewer opportunities for building my resume. Could I really afford to sacrifice everything this organization had given me?

Instead, my focus was on the handful of men who had left as a result of the hazing practices and the others in the future who could avoid those practices if I just held my ground.

With my eyes focused not on myself, but on the people I was hoping to help, I knew I could make it through that defining moment because focusing on something greater than ourselves equips us with extraordinary powers.

And nowhere is that more evident than in the examples of our world's youngest heroes.

THE REASON

From Ruby Bridges in the United States, to Nkosi Johnson in South Africa, and to Thandiwe Chama in Zambia, children throughout the world have faced obstacles and oppression in their quest for access to education.

However, few examples are as dramatic and powerful as that of Malala Yousafzai. In 2009, a then-eleven-year-old Yousafzai began blogging for the British Broadcasting Corporation with an entry beginning, "I am afraid."

"I was afraid going to school because the Taleban had issued an edict banning all girls from attending schools," Yousafzai wrote. "Only eleven students attended the class out of twenty-seven. The number decreased because of Taleban's edict."

Over the days, weeks, and years to come, Yousafzai became the face and voice of a movement. In 2011, she received Pakistan's first National Youth Peace Prize, and she was nominated by Archbishop Desmond Tutu for the International Children's Peace Prize.

At a time when the Pakistani government had backed down and ceded large chunks of land to the Taliban, this child's courage was even more astonishing.

But the Taliban, which abhorred Yousafzai's high profile and public stand against it, made a move to silence the young activist for good.

In her book, *I Am Malala*, Yousafzai acknowledges she and her father were aware of the Taliban's threats against them, and her father even suggested she end her campaign and public protests. She responded, "How can we do that? You were the one who said that if we believe in something greater than our lives, then our voices will only multiply even if we are dead. We can't disown our campaign!"

In spite of the threats against her very life, her focus remained on those she was working to help. She stayed focused on her reason for speaking up.

On October 9, 2012, a masked gunman boarded her school bus and demanded to know which of the children on board was Yousafzai, threatening to shoot all of them if Yousafzai did not reveal herself.

When she was identified, Yousafzai was shot with a single bullet that traveled through her head, neck, and shoulder. Yousafzai remained in a coma for nine days and was hospitalized for nearly three months.

After all of this, Yousafzai remained focused on the reason for her fight.

In a July 12, 2013, speech to the United Nations, she said, "The terrorists thought they would change my aims and stop my ambitions, but nothing changed in my life except this: weakness, fear, and hopelessness died. Strength, power, and courage was born.... I am not against anyone, neither am I here to speak in terms of personal revenge against the Taliban or any other terrorist group. I'm here to speak up for the right of education for every child. I want education for the sons and daughters of the Taliban and all terrorists and extremists."

The next year, at the age of seventeen, she received the Nobel Peace Prize, becoming the world's youngest Nobel laureate.

EXERCISE

In this chapter, we entered the Innermost Cave, where our deepest, darkest fears reside. Thinking about the causes or issues you care about most and your own heroic journey, what are your fears?

Consider what monsters may be lurking on your path. Are there people or situations you avoid? Are there facts, histories, ideas, or situations you don't want others to hear or see? What do you, your organization, or your community hide or actively avoid?

_____

_____

_____

Conversely, what people or situations do you fight or resist? In what situations or with what kinds of people do you find yourself becoming frustrated or maybe even outright defiant?

_____

_____

_____

Now that you've identified the people and situations in which you either Forget Everything And Run or Face Everything And Rise, in what ways can you find compassion and empathy with others? How can you Focus on Empathy, Adventure, and Rational thinking to help and serve others?

_____

_____

_____

SUMMARY

Fear is more than a physical response; it is a force. The longer we allow our fears to live within us, the greater and more powerful they become. This is why, in our imaginations, the scariest monsters lurk in the shadows, away from any inspection or evaluation.

Fortunately, our physiology also offers us the power to overcome our fears. By focusing not on ourselves and our own self-preservation, but on our opportunities to help and serve others, we find extraordinary power within us.

CHAPTER 17

FALLING ON YOUR FACE

"You may have a fresh start any moment you choose, for this thing that we call 'failure' is not the falling down, but the staying down."

— Mary Pickford

Every eye in the room was on me.

After all of the questions had been asked, and after all of the answers had been given, the opportunity to compete for the National Geographic State Geography Bee championship had come down to one last question.

In the semifinal round in Omaha, Nebraska, after more than an hour of back-and-forth competition, my opponent and I were tied. Each of us had been given the tiebreaker question, and each of us would have the opportunity to respond. If one of us answered correctly and the other did not, the semifinal round would end, and the person who answered correctly would go on to the final round, which would be broadcast on statewide TV.

The man who had been my grade school teacher from fourth through eighth grade was sitting in the front row of the crowded room. As the tiebreaker question was asked, I could see the building elation on Mr. Mattek's face. He knew there was no way I would get the question wrong. Not only had we prepared and studied together for months, but because our school was so small, Mr. Mattek had been my teacher for every class over those five years.

The moderator's question echoed through an otherwise nervous, tension-filled room.

"In what city is the Temple of the Parthenon?"

As my mind raced, one clear thought soon rose to the surface. After spending the previous eight years in a small Christian school, I knew of only one place where one of the world's greatest temples could be located.

"Jerusalem," I answered enthusiastically.

Almost as soon as the first syllable left my lips, Mr. Mattek's face fell into his hands. At that moment, even before my opponent gave his answer, I knew the competition was over for me.

By the time the other contestant correctly answered, "Athens, Greece," I already was preparing for a very long, very disappointing sixty-minute drive home.

I had failed in a public, somewhat humiliating way, and it took quite a few years for me to live down the stories that followed that moment. In fact, the next time I see Mr. Mattek, I have no doubt that story will still be among the very first he will eagerly retell.

In the last two chapters, you confronted the first of the three Fs: your foes and your fears. Our foes are the external forces we fight, whereas fear and failure make up the internal forces we fight.

Now we turn to the third of the three Fs—the ever-present potential for failure.

FAILURE AS FAULT

At some time in our hero's journey, and even more likely multiple times in our journey, we all will fail. Failure is an inevitable, yet uncomfortable and unwelcome companion on our journey. When we encounter failure, we lash out and react with strong emotions. We may blame others for our failures. We may claim small wins or moral victories, settling for less than the heights of our original vision. We may even rename our failures with euphemisms and platitudes. We do these things just to make the demoralizing, discomforting, and otherwise distasteful experience of failure more acceptable and tolerable.

But the truth is, whether it is in the beginning, middle, or end of our journey, we all fall flat on our faces from time to time. It's painful; it stings. But if we so choose, it also will stick with us.

In our journeys, and indeed in every part of our lives, we face failures. In some cases, those failures are our fault. We either do the wrong things or we do not do the right things. At other times, failure finds us. Circumstances and situations conspire against us, and we fall.

As I fought hazing in my organization, I made my share of mistakes. I'm not talking about doing everything the best I could, but nonetheless falling short. I'm talking about glaring, unforgivable wrongs for which I alone was responsible.

Because of my role as scholarship chairman for my organization, I was responsible for organizing study nights for the pledge class. During one of those study nights, I read to all of them the fraternity's national policy and the university's policy against hazing, as I shared in Chapter 7. I finished that meeting by promising them, "If you ever feel scared, threatened, or uncomfortable, come to our room, and you will be safe."

After a few weeks, when I saw nobody was taking me up on my offer to find sanctuary in our room, I decided I needed to show them I was watching out for them.

I saw a chance for my demonstration as the organization planned its next line-up, where it would awaken the pledge class at three or four in the morning with screaming, while banging pots and pans and blaring air horns. Then it would hustle them down the stairs to the basement, where the pledges would be punished and ridiculed before being sent off to do calisthenics, house cleaning, or whatever meaningless task the organization had in mind.

On the night of that next line-up, I decided I would show the pledge class my support by showing up at the line-up as well, but remaining in the background. I did not participate in any way, but I know in hindsight that my presence there was a silent endorsement of the hazing they were enduring.

I had promised to keep them safe and protect them, but I stood there and said nothing as they were threatened and tormented. This was one of my first failures in my fight against hazing, but my biggest failure was yet to come.

A few weeks later, another member and I were discussing the midterm grade reports we had received for the pledges. Their academic performance was faltering, so it was my role to light the proverbial fire beneath them and push them to perform to a higher standard.

It was already relatively late, and the entire pledge class was asleep in the dorm. Suddenly, without any warning, I burst into the room and began screaming at the pledges at the top of my lungs. I don't remember a single word of what I said. All I remember is that I was alone with them in that room, and I never turned on the lights.

For me, it was easier to confront them in the dark because I could not see how any of them reacted to or felt about what I said. I could imagine myself yelling into the darkness without giving any thought to how I was hurting any of them.

I may have made a mistake in the first example, but my second failure was nothing short of a catastrophic collapse. In all of the years I have fought, researched, and spoken out against hazing, I have never forgotten those failures, and they have driven me in powerful ways.

Our failures ache and burn, but they also linger. They can teach us in ways that success never will. Those failures become the hard-earned lessons we carry with us long after the memories of our triumphs fade.

Robin Sharma, a motivational speaker and best-selling author, said, "There are no mistakes in life, only lessons. There is no such thing as a negative experience, only opportunities to grow, learn, and advance along the road of self-mastery. From struggle comes strength. Even pain can be a wonderful teacher."

When failure inevitably finds us, we must find the growth and lesson contained therein.

But let's be clear. No matter how nobly we approach failure, the process can be an absolute mess, and we may feel like we're disappointing everyone who cares about us.

FAILURE AS FALLING SHORT

In Chapter 6, I described how I often try to connect with authors who inspire me. In 2012, one of my followers on social media recommended I watch a movie titled *Finding Joe*.

I never could have anticipated how deeply this film would resonate with me. By 6:39 p.m. that same night, I had already reached out to Patrick Takaya Solomon, the film's producer and director. In the years since, we have continued to exchange messages from time to time.

One of my favorite parts of the movie is Solomon's interview with Brian Johnson. In his interview, Johnson describes his experience of falling short of others' expectations, not just once, but twice, and in both cases, in dramatic and very significant ways.

Shortly after graduating from the University of California-Los Angeles with a degree in business and psychology, Johnson went to work at Arthur Anderson & Co., doing accounting, financial planning, and consulting work.

Despite having what may seem like a dream job at a dream company, Johnson said he literally threw up on his way home from work in his first week. He left Arthur Anderson & Co. shortly thereafter.

He applied to, was accepted, and began studying at the University of California, Berkeley, law school, one of the best law schools in the world.

However, it still wasn't right. He said he couldn't even make it through the first semester. What would you do if you had one of the most sought-after jobs in the world but hated it? And then, even more than that, what if you had left one prestigious job, were then admitted to one of the most renowned graduate programs in the world, and hated that, too? Would you have the courage to leave such a charmed life—not only once, but twice?

Not only that, but imagine you also were in a relationship with someone attending medical school at an Ivy League college. What would others think of you if you said, "Thanks, but no thanks," to all of those things and moved back home to live with your parents?

Johnson said goodbye to all of those things.

As he let go of all these things in his life, he understandably found himself "spinning"—his entire life felt like a train wreck.

"It is the most challenging parts of our lives," Johnson said, "when we look back at them with a deep enough perspective, that we see those were the best moments of our lives. Without them, we wouldn't be who we are."

In that far-from-desirable state, Johnson found his inspiration and his path. In that dark moment of his life, Johnson said the only thing he knew he wanted to do was coach a little league baseball team. Before long, that tiny impulse led to an idea to serve kids through sports. Once he had this inspiration, his plan took off. Johnson won the business plan competition at UCLA, raised $5 million, and grew the business to forty-five employees in less than nine months. He even hired the CEO of Adidas to be Eteamz, Inc.'s CEO.

Johnson recognizes now that he had to go through the struggles and challenges to find his true path.

In the words of Joseph Campbell, "We must be willing to get rid of the life we've planned, so as to have the life that is waiting for us."

Once we are ready to risk disappointing others or making a mistake along the way, we have set the foundation for achieving something greater than ourselves.

FAILURE AS FOUNDATION

Ask almost anyone to list the greatest presidents in US history and you'll find Abraham Lincoln very close to the top of that list. But if you were to inventory the presidents who endured the most failure in their lives, you might be surprised that Lincoln would also be atop that list.

For Lincoln, the failures were early and often. In 1816, when Lincoln was just seven years old, his family moved from Kentucky to Indiana due to a dispute about his family's title to the land.

Just two years later, in 1818, Lincoln's mother died, leaving his eleven-year-old sister, Sarah, in charge of the household. Sarah herself passed away in 1828, while giving birth to a stillborn son. In 1830, Lincoln helped his father establish a farm in Illinois, before setting out on his own.

Lincoln's setbacks were hardly limited to his personal life. After losing his job in 1831, he finished eighth out of thirteen contenders for a seat in the Illinois state legislature in 1832. He followed up that loss by starting, and sinking, his own business in 1833, which drove him deeply into debt.

Fortune finally smiled on Lincoln in 1834, when he was elected to the Illinois state legislature on his second try. But after a brief respite, tragedy again found Lincoln the next year when Ann Rutledge, with whom he was in a relationship, died from typhoid fever at the age of twenty-two. Rutledge's passing caused Lincoln to fall into a deep depression.

In the end, even though today he is widely recognized as one of the greatest politicians of all time, nine times he was denied for a variety of roles at every level of public service. For any person to have endured so many personal and professional setbacks and then become one of the greatest heroes of all time is miraculous. To be clear, Lincoln's journey to the top was not one in which he bounded from one failure to the next. He was brought to his knees on several occasions, but he did not allow those setbacks to keep him on his knees for long.

"My great concern is not whether you have failed, but whether you are content with your failure," he said.

When we get knocked down, it can be easy to give up. "At least we tried." But especially in those trying times, we cannot be content with our failures, but rather we must *contend* with them.

EXERCISE

Sir Winston Churchill, Prime Minister of the United Kingdom, who helped lead the Allied forces to victory in World War II, said, "Success is not final, failure is not fatal: it is the courage to continue that counts." In what areas of your life have you failed?

_____

_____

_____

How have you grown and learned through those experiences? How have you become a stronger person as a result of those times when you have failed or struggled?

_____

_____

_____

In thinking about the causes or issues you care about most, in what ways might you experience failure? What mistakes might you make? In what ways might you disappoint your family, your friends, or others around you?

_____

_____

_____

SUMMARY

You will fall short. You will make mistakes. You will fail. Although some of us will fight tooth and nail to avoid failure, it is inevitable and unavoidable. But it is not the end; it is simply a step in the process.

What do you do when a piece of pottery breaks? Do you throw it out? In the traditional Japanese art of kintsugi, a precious metal, such as gold or silver, is liquefied and inserted into the breaks and cracks, which not only restores the broken item, but gives it a new and unique feature.

The brokenness and the failure are no longer the end, but a new, stronger beginning. We all fall, but our decision to rise is what makes us heroes.

CHAPTER 18

RESOLVING TO RISE

"Resilience is very different than being numb. Resilience means you experience, you feel, you fail, you hurt. You fall. But, you keep going."

— Yasmin Mogahed

Have you ever gone searching for treasure? Maybe as a child you dug a few holes in the backyard of your home, or maybe, like me, you day-dreamed of finding a pirate's treasure in a remote and secluded part of your hometown.

My oldest son has a box of treasures in his room. Whenever we go to a park or playground, or just out for a walk, he looks for interesting and somewhat exceptional items to take back home with him. The box contains everything from a broken cassette tape and an old padlock to discarded firework parachutes and a pile of nuts and bolts. When we are young, we can be captivated by dreams of buried treasure, but for two brothers from Michigan, those dreams have become a quest.

One of my favorite shows is *The Curse of Oak Island*. For five seasons and counting, Marty and Rick Lagina have spent millions of dollars trying to find and unearth a legendary, centuries-old treasure alleged to be lying somewhere on an island in Nova Scotia, Canada. The purported location of the treasure is known as the "Money Pit," perhaps more for the fortunes sunk into centuries of treasure hunts than for whatever may lie there.

Season after season, the brothers come to the island overflowing with optimism, only to face setback after setback. The costs of excavation and exploration mount, promising leads disappear, tunnels flood, and even successful digs and dives become dead ends. The more they dig, the more dead ends they find, but they keep trying, season after season.

As each of us travels our own hero's journey, we encounter the dead ends of our foes, our fears, and our failures. In the last three chapters, we have explored these obstacles to our success. Now we must resolve to rise above the walls that block our paths.

OPENING DOORS

Can you imagine the frustration the Laginas feel every time they invest their energy, money, and time into their project, only to fail to find any fruits for their labors?

Chances are you have experienced that type of frustration, maybe not on the same scale but in sentiment. Maybe you are a college student who participated in a transformational leadership opportunity this year, and now you're struggling with how to bring positive change to your organization.

Or maybe you are a young professional who is contemplating a career change, but you don't know whether your skills will transfer to a new field, and you're afraid of "starting over."

Perhaps you are a quarter-lifer thinking about the big questions of meaning and purpose in your life, but the challenges and problems you see in your community and throughout the world are overwhelming.

Regardless of the type of wall you're facing, you know how daunting it is to look up, look down, and look to each side, only to see no way out.

Where do you even start?

Fortunately, Joseph Campbell, author of *The Hero with a Thousand Faces*, offers us more than hope. He offers us a way forward. "Follow your bliss and the universe will open doors for you where there were only walls."

How do we "follow our bliss?" The first clue is that—whatever it is—our bliss makes us come alive. It drives us. It energizes us. It makes our hearts race.

"We're not on our journey to save the world but to save ourselves. But in doing that you save the world. The influence of a vital person vitalizes," Campbell said.

The second clue is that following our bliss scares us. Our fears are the price of admission.

"You enter the forest at the darkest point, where there is no path," Campbell said. "Where there is a way or path, it is someone else's path. You are not on your own path. If you follow someone else's way, you are not going to realize your potential."

The answer, the only response, really, is to act, even if it is to take the smallest step.

Hope is the result of action, not the cause. We do not act because we have hope; we have hope because we act. Often, we feel the most stuck when we think we've tried everything. The truth is there almost always is at least one more option, one more person to talk to, or one more route to try. It may be audacious and scary, and we may not see a clear path, but that is precisely why it will work. It is our path and no one else's. A path that does not belong to us will not take us where we want to go. It is someone else's path.

By following someone else's path, a shortcut, we cut short our own potential. At best, we will become a second-rate version of someone else.

If we want to become our best, we cannot follow someone else's path. Our best is ours and ours alone. The foes, fears, and failures along the way are there to forge and shape us. And eventually, to deliver us to our destination, so long as we demonstrate the drive to follow our own path.

EXERCISE

Consider what "following your bliss" would look like for you. What makes you come alive? What makes your heart race? What makes your heart sing?

_____

_____

_____

When you think about following your bliss, what part of it is scary for you? What doubts do you have? What makes you nervous?

_____

_____

_____

What are one, two, or three small steps you could take to address some of those fears, to eliminate some of those doubts, or to make you feel less nervous?

_____

_____

_____

DRIVING FORWARD

Once upon a time, a young man wanted to know the secret of success in life. The young man spent years studying every successful person who had ever lived. But the more he studied them, the farther away success seemed.

One day, as the young man was about to give up hope, he heard about a guru who lived in a remote part of the world. This guru not only knew the secret of success, but it was said that every single person who had learned the guru's secret had indeed found success.

With this near-guarantee in mind, the young man set about finding the guru.

Now this guru lived in complete isolation at the top of a mountain. The young man, determined to meet with the guru, eagerly embarked on the journey. He was determined to reach the top, overcoming every obstacle along the way. He cut his way through thick underbrush, climbed over bulging and jagged rocks, fought back wild beasts, and at long last reached the top of the mountain.

At the top of the mountain, exhausted from his arduous journey, he flopped onto his back, gasping for air. As he took in his surroundings, he glimpsed the guru only a few feet away, deep in meditation.

Being a polite person and desiring to be respectful of the guru's meditation time, the young man became aware of his gulping breaths and stifled them as much as possible until his breathing returned to normal.

Lying there at the top of the mountain, the seconds became minutes, and the minutes gave way to hours. The young man waited.

When the guru opened his eyes, he stood up and turned toward the young man.

"I have come a great distance in search of the secret of life," the young man said.

But the guru did not reply. He simply began walking down a narrow path on the side of the mountain. The young man decided he should follow him.

The young man found it difficult to keep pace with the older man, who skipped from one rock to the next with the agility of a mountain goat. They walked for more than an hour, and the young man began to wonder where they were going.

Just then, they reached a clearing. There, set among the surrounding mountains was a lake, as clear as crystal. The waters were smooth and still, with the surface glinting softly in the sun's reflection.

The guru approached the edge of the lake and beckoned the young man closer. With a gesture, he asked him to kneel down.

Sensing he would soon know the long-sought-after secret of life, the young man eagerly followed the guru's instructions.

Suddenly, he felt a strong and swift force at the back of his neck. Without warning, the guru had grabbed the back of the young man's head and forced it beneath the water's surface.

This is some kind of test, said the man to himself, as he regained his composure.

After a minute passed, the young man began doubting that he could hold his breath much longer. The grip on his neck was no weaker than before. After another minute crept by, he was about to panic. His heart beat with bigger and faster thuds against his chest, and his lungs screamed for air.

If I start to struggle, the guru will know I need to stop to breathe, the young man thought.

The young man moved his feet and pressed against the older man's grip, but the guru pressed harder and tightened his grip, forcing the young man even farther into the water.

Now, the young man was desperate. He began swinging his arms and legs wildly in every direction. He could no longer trust the guru to let him go, so he would try to escape by any means possible. But the more the young man thrashed, the tighter the older man held on.

Finally, the young man began to black out. His arms and legs became so weak that they flopped at his sides, and his brain seemed to flicker in and out of consciousness.

This is it, he thought. *I'm going to die.*

With that thought, the young man accepted he would die right there, face down in the lake.

And at that very moment, the guru let go.

The young man leapt away from the guru and onto the shore, gasping for air. As precious oxygen flooded into his lungs, his vision became clearer and clearer, and his arms and legs steadied beneath him as he crouched there on the shore. But his gratitude for air and for life soon turned into boiling hostility toward the guru.

He jumped up and charged toward the guru, screaming, "Are you crazy? You could have killed me!"

Calmly, the guru stared back at the young man, watching his chest heave up and down with each angry breath. Then the guru opened his mouth for the first time, speaking gently.

"When your head was under water, what did you want to do?"

"I wanted to breathe!" the young man yelled back.

"You asked for the secret of success. Here it is. When you want success as much as you wanted to breathe, then, and only then, will you have success."

Without saying another word, the guru turned around and walked away.

As we go through our lives, we will face countless obstacles and walls, but it is our determination to keep moving forward that will make all the difference.

In thinking about the story of the guru and the young man, you can find two lessons for yourself and your own journey. The first, and most obvious, lesson is that when you want success as badly as you want to breathe, you will find it. It will never be easy—it may even be painful and scary—but if you want it badly enough, you will find it.

The second, less obvious lesson, is that when you are living your journey, you may find that your being and your breath is all you have left. Even in that most desperate situation, you can always move forward with hope.

SURVIVING FORWARD

Few people can demonstrate the simple hope of moving forward better than Norman Ollestad, author of *Crazy for the Storm*, and the sole survivor of a horrific plane crash.

At 8:00 a.m. on February 19, 1979, a chartered Cessna aircraft carrying four people crashed into the San Gabriel Mountains in southern California. The pilot and one passenger perished in the crash, leaving an eleven-year-old boy, Ollestad, and the boy's father's girlfriend, Sandra Cressman, as the only survivors.

After huddling together for warmth beneath one of the plane's wings for several hours and fearing they might freeze to death in blizzard conditions while more than 8,200 feet up a rugged mountain, Ollestad and Cressman decided the best option for survival was to make their way down the mountain.

As they began their trek, Cressman soon fell down an icy chute and perished, leaving the young boy completely on his own several thousand feet up the mountain.

At one point during his descent, Ollestad saw a helicopter fly overhead and he stood to wave. He said in an interview for *The New York Times* the following day. "It looked like they saw me, but I guess they didn't, and they never came back."

Can you imagine Ollestad's disappointment and heartbreak in that situation? After crashing into a mountain and losing his father, he loses the only other person who survived the crash. Then, as he is making his way down the mountain by himself, he sees a helicopter—a potential rescue—only to have that hope disappear over the horizon.

"I never gave up. Dad taught me to never give up."

Ollestad alternated hiking and stop-and-go sliding as he descended the mountain. In his 1979 interview, he said, "I was just sliding down on my butt and every time I got going too fast, I stuck a stick in the snow."

After trekking two miles from the crash site, Ollestad reached the bottom of the mountain, where he was able to follow a small creek to a ranch house. The people there were able to call for help.

Ollestad credits much of his survival to his father, who he said conditioned him from an early age "to feel comfortable in the storm." His father pushed him to confront his fears, whether riding a dangerous and threatening wave on the beach or taking on the most challenging ski slope on the mountain. He never let his son give up.

We may say that Ollestad's father taught him resilience. But for Ollestad, it was nothing short of survival.

THRIVING THROUGH HOPE

Do you feel even just a little bit intimidated by Ollestad's story? Do you wonder how you could summon the resolve and strength he showed as an eleven-year-old boy?

Courage and hope are not always things we find inside ourselves. Sometimes, we find them in others, or others find them in us.

Perhaps no person in history exemplified this truth more than Fred Rogers, known throughout the world as Mister Rogers, the gentle, honest, and optimistic man who welcomed children worldwide to his TV neighborhood for almost forty years—and whose program continued in syndication for more years than that.

Rogers was a musician, pilot, producer, puppeteer, writer, and ordained minister, in addition to serving as the host for his well-known show.

In his book, *Life's Journeys According to Mister Rogers*, Rogers seems to be speaking directly to those of us who may be intimated by the courage and resolve demonstrated by Ollestad on that mountain.

"We'd all like to feel self-reliant and capable of coping with whatever adversity comes our way, but that's not how most human beings are made. It's my belief that the capacity to accept help is inseparable from the capacity to give help when our turn comes to be strong," Rogers wrote.

In those really challenging, really intimidating times, it can be tough to ask for the help and support we need, but when we have someone we can count on, we can find the strength to continue moving forward.

As I confronted my fraternity's hazing practices, I experienced this truth firsthand. The night I was ambushed inside the chapter's meeting room and compelled to read the emails I had sent detailing the organization's hazing practices, I certainly did not feel courageous or hopeful.

More than anything, I felt scared.

After everything that had happened, I knew I couldn't even sleep in my own bed that night. Imagine that. For nearly two years, I had called those men my brothers, yet I couldn't even trust them with my physical safety. It was nearly 1:00 a.m., and I had no idea what to do.

The men, who just a few minutes before had ambushed me, screamed at me, and even threatened my life, would soon be emerging from the meeting room. What would they do?

Although I had no faith in the bonds of brotherhood I once shared with those men, there was no question whom I could count on to help me.

I immediately called Chris, my friend and mentor from Theta Chi, whom I mentioned in Chapter 6. I said to him, "Can you come pick me up? I need to move out now."

As Chris hung up the phone, he asked his roommate, Joe Kopp, whether he could borrow his truck. Before Joe said yes, he asked what Chris needed his truck for in the middle of the night. "Chad needs to move out," Chris said.

"Can I come?" Joe asked.

Then, as the two of them were leaving their house, their third roommate, Trevor Johnson, asked where they were going so late. "Chad needs to move out," they said.

"Can I come?" Trevor asked.

A few minutes after I had called for help, Chris, Joe, and Trevor, who all were members of Theta Chi, the first fraternity I had left when it closed for financial reasons, entered the fraternity house where I was living. It seemed like a scene from a movie. As Chris, Joe, and Trevor came in, the men who had cornered me in the meeting room emerged from their meeting and began lining the hallways, saying all sorts of things to intimidate and scare my friends and me.

So much of my life at that time was ending: long-held friendships, my living situation, my membership with that organization. These three men, however, provided the help and support I needed at that time. They gave me the hope I could not have found on my own in that moment.

"Often when you think you're at the end of something, you're at the beginning of something else," Rogers said. "Transitions are almost always signs of growth, but they can bring feelings of loss. To get somewhere new, we may have to leave somewhere else behind."

As we go through our own journeys, it can be easy to focus on what is going wrong or what we are losing in the process, but hope is the belief that a better future is possible—and that we have the power to make it real.

EXERCISE

In those moments when it is difficult for us to find our own hope, we can look to others to give us hope. In Ollestad's story, it was his father who helped him look inside and find the hope he needed in that dark moment. In my own story, it was Chris, Joe, and Trevor willingly taking on a hostile and intimidating situation to help me.

What past influences can you look to for strength and support in difficult times? Who can guide, help, and support you?

_____

_____

_____

When things are at their worst, the only solution is to move forward. Without movement, we are stuck. Hope is the result of action, not the cause. What small steps can you take to gain positive momentum when you are stuck?

_____

_____

_____

SUMMARY

In the last chapter, we discussed the inevitability and unavoidability of failure in our hero's journey, as well as in our everyday lives. Our resolve to rise from those failures is what makes the difference.

In the movie *Justice League*, the world faces the death of Superman, who bears an "S"-like symbol on his chest, the Kryptonian symbol for "hope." The movie closes with a line from Lois Lane, who was engaged to the fallen hero:

"The world has grown darker. And while we have reason to fear, we have the strength not to. There are heroes among us, to remind us that only from fear, comes courage; that only from darkness, can we truly feel the light."

When we fall, as we inevitably will time and time again, we find the courage, the resolve, and the strength to rise. We learn that our failures are not the end, but rather a new, more powerful, more promising, and more hopeful beginning.

CHAPTER 19

BREAKING THROUGH

"It is from numberless diverse acts of courage and belief...
that human history is thus shaped. Each time a person stands
up for an ideal, or acts to improve the lot of others, or strikes
out against injustice, he sends forth a tiny ripple of hope, and
crossing each other from a million different centers of energy
and daring, those ripples build a current which can sweep
down the mightiest walls of oppression and resistance."

— Robert F. Kennedy

Have you ever traveled to a truly ancient city?

Here in the United States, it is hard to find edifices and structures that
are more than a few hundred years old, so when I traveled to London,
Mexico City, and Rome, I was struck by the way those sprawling me-
tropolises sit on top of and within their ancient foundations.

One of the clearest examples is St. Peter's Basilica in Vatican City.

According to tradition, St. Peter was martyred between 64 and 68 CE.
In the following years, a sepulchral monument was built over the top
of St. Peter's underground tomb.

For nearly 250 years thereafter, Christians living in and around Rome suffered extreme persecution, so any veneration of St. Peter's tomb was done in absolute secrecy—tradition states that his remains and many of the outward markers of his tomb may have been removed during the most severe periods of persecution.

Then, in the fourth century, Constantine the Great assumed control of the Roman Empire. He not only brought an end to the persecution of the early Christian church, but he ordered the construction of a five-aisled basilica atop the historical location of St. Peter's tomb.

When a second St. Peter's Basilica was built between 1506 and 1626, the new structure was built on the same site. What is most remarkable about the history of this site is that when you descend into the catacombs of the necropolis beneath the main altar in St. Peter's Basilica, you can see all four of these iterations, beginning at the bottom with the memorial first built above the tomb, with each successive structure built directly on top of the one before.

As a modern American, I find it absolutely awe-inspiring to see the magnificence of the modern St. Peter's Basilica and Square on the outside and its progression from a relatively humble and simple structure on the inside.

Couldn't we say the same for ourselves and our own hero's journey? When we embark on our journey, we are "in it to win it." We have in our hearts a big, beautiful vision of the change we want to make in our organizations, our communities, and our world. And from the seemingly simple beginnings of a dream or vision, the impact of our work can grow to the grandest scale.

Personally, my vision was not just to end hazing in my organization, but to eradicate it from the entire world. Was it a realistic vision? Maybe, or maybe not. But was it a vision worth pursuing? Absolutely.

In TV shows and movies, we watch heroes make a world of difference in a span of just a few minutes, moving mountains in less time than it takes for many of us to move a piece of heavy furniture. In our journeys, our breakthroughs are likely to be more "baby steps" than "giant leaps," but to paraphrase Hungarian essayist and novelist George Konrad, courageous change "is only the accumulation of small steps."

THE PROCESS

On November 7, 1998, a mediocre team led by a mediocre head coach changed college football. Nick Saban, who was at that time a coach with a 23-20 career record and was coaching a team with a 4-4 record that year, introduced a mindset that would lead his overwhelmingly underdog Michigan State Spartans to an upset win over the number one-ranked and undefeated Ohio State Buckeyes in Columbus, Ohio.

Today, Saban is one of the most accomplished coaches in college football history, having won six national championships, including five of the last nine. All of his success, Saban says, has stemmed from the approach he implemented in that game against a heavily favored Ohio State team, an approach he refers to simply as "The Process."

But what is "The Process?"

Saban said:

> We decided to use the approach that we're not going to focus on the outcome. We were just going to focus on the process of what it took to play the best football you could play, which was to focus on that particular play as if it had a history and life of its own.

> Don't look at the scoreboard, don't look at any external factors, just all your focus and all your concentration, all your effort, all your toughness, all your discipline to execute went into that particular play. Regardless of what happened on that play, success or failure, you would move on to the next play and have the same focus to do that on the next play, and you'd then do that for sixty minutes in a game and then you'd be able to live with the results regardless of what those results were.

In every moment, focus on doing your best in that moment. Not the last moment. Not the next moment. The moment in front of you. By winning each of those moments, one by one, plays are won, series are won, quarters are won, games are won, and in the end, championships are won.

It can feel overwhelming to look at your vision, to see the proverbial mountain you want to move and to think you will never make a difference. *Maybe someday,* you think, *when I have more courage, more energy, more time, etc., I will move that mountain.*

"Someday" is today.

Whatever it is you want to become, become that the best you can in this moment. Whatever it is you want to do, do that the best you can in this moment.

By focusing on what we can do—big or small—in this moment right now, we begin moving the mountain one rock at a time.

Sometimes, we even find others who are willing to help us move those rocks.

EXERCISE

"The Process" allows us to be our best and to give our best in the present moment, whether that is the next fifteen minutes or the next fifteen seconds. The only way to build your dream and follow your journey is by accepting and acting on the opportunity of this moment in time, right now.

How will you implement "The Process" in your own hero's journey? When you do so, what will happen as a result?

_____

_____

_____

How will you implement "The Process" in your family life? What will the outcome be?

_____

_____

_____

How will you implement "The Process" in your career? What will the result be?

_____

_____

_____

In what other areas can you implement "The Process?" How will you do that? What changes will happen as a result?

_____

_____

_____

THE RIDE

In 1900, the city of Montgomery, Alabama, passed an ordinance to segregate bus passengers by race, with white passengers having seats in the front of the bus and black passengers having seats in the back. By law, no passengers could be forced to give up their seats, but by practice, black passengers often were forced to move to accommodate white passengers. More than that, if white people were already sitting in the front of the bus, black people had to enter the front of the bus, pay the fare, then exit the bus and reenter through the rear door.

One day in 1943, Rosa Parks boarded the bus. Although you may be familiar with Parks' story, you probably don't know that after paying her fare on this day, she was told to disembark the bus and reenter through the rear door. As soon as Parks exited the bus, the driver drove off without her.

Over the next few years, Irene Morgan, Lillie Mae Bradford, Sarah Louise Keys, Aurelia Browder, Claudette Colvin, Susie McDonald, Mary Louise Smith, Jeanetta Reese, and others resisted bus segregation in Alabama, North Carolina, and Virginia.

While it was Browder, Colvin, McDonald, and Smith's successful lawsuit in 1956, that ultimately ended bus segregation in Montgomery and throughout the state of Alabama, it was Parks' refusal to give up her seat on December 1, 1955—twelve long years after that bus drove off without her—that became a galvanizing symbol for the modern Civil Rights Movement.

After Parks' arrest, where she was charged with "failing to obey orders of bus driver," the Women's Political Council began calling for a December 5 boycott of the Montgomery bus system, the date of Parks' trial in municipal court.

As 40,000 riders boycotted the bus the day of Parks' trial, the newly formed Montgomery Improvement Association elected twenty-six-year-old pastor Dr. Martin Luther King, Jr. to serve as its first president. Shortly after the end of the Montgomery Bus Boycott, King went on to help found the Southern Christian Leadership Conference, which would establish him as one of the greatest civil rights leaders of all time.

Parks, who is often misrepresented as an exhausted seamstress who was too tired to give up her seat, was in fact actively involved in the Civil Rights Movement, having been elected secretary for the Montgomery chapter of the National Association for the Advancement of

Colored People (NAACP) in December 1943.

In her autobiography, *My Story*, Parks wrote, "People always say that I didn't give up my seat because I was tired, but that isn't true. I was not tired physically, or no more tired than I usually was at the end of a working day…. No, the only tired I was, was tired of giving in."

Parks and all of the women before her undoubtedly were persistent, and by each of them contributing her best to the movement, they not only moved one mountain for one city in Alabama, but through their example and by giving King a place in the national spotlight, they were able to help move many mountains in cities throughout the United States.

To be sure, it was a very difficult, very long journey from the beginning of Montgomery, Alabama's bus segregation laws and practices in 1900 to their end on December 20, 1956. The consistent and persistent resistance demonstrated by Parks proves that the greatest changes come one step at a time.

When you think about how very difficult and how very long their journey was, you may wonder about those who protested and resisted in the early years who did not live to see the desegregation of Montgomery's buses.

In situations where we do not get to see the benefits of our efforts, we still receive a reward for our work.

EXERCISE

Parks and every other woman who resisted segregation in the Montgomery bus system experienced those injustices day in and day out at a time when those laws and practices were powerful social norms. It would have been easy to accept them as just "the way things are." After all, their day-to-day lives got even harder as a result of their resistance, yet they fought for the cause and the rights they believed in.

What injustices do you see around you? They may be things you experience yourself, or they may be things you see others experience.

_____

_____

_____

We often see standing up against injustice as a big, bold act, but it can be as simple as sitting still, as evidenced by Parks and the lunch counter sit-ins in Greensboro, North Carolina. What are some simple ways you could send a clear message about the injustices you identified above?

_____

_____

_____

Although Parks' refusal to move was one of the sparks that ignited the Civil Rights Movement, it also was a culmination of previous protests and acts of resistance. In what ways can you add your voice and your actions to existing movements to move them forward? To whose legacy can you contribute?

_____

_____

_____

THE REWARD

At the beginning of the hero's journey, in Chapter 4, you set out to get something, to have something, or to make a difference in your group, community, or world. The journey introduced you to your mentors, taught you about your allies and foes, and tested and prepared you for your greatest challenges.

In Chapters 16 and 17, you came face to face with your darkest fears and ever-lurking failures.

The best and most satisfying things in life follow our struggles. After all, we appreciate gifts, but we truly treasure those things we earn.

After everything you have gone through along your journey, you may be expecting to read that this is the moment when you finally find success. This is the moment when it all pays off; this is the moment when you receive the reward for your work.

But that is not always the case.

For some of us, our reward is a magnificent outcome we could not have imagined.

In the previous chapters, I shared my story of fighting hazing in my organization. In Chapter 18, I shared my story of emerging from a chapter meeting room late at night, scared for my own wellbeing, and reaching out to Chris, Trevor, and Joe to move me out in the middle of the night.

When I stepped out of the meeting room at the end of my ordeal, I was aware I had sacrificed my chance to be a member of that organization in exchange for standing up for a cause I deeply believed in.

Before that night, I had envisioned a time when our organization would become a brilliant example of a group that had changed its ways and a gold standard for other chapters on campus and across the country.

Before that night, I thought a growing number of people within the organization—if brought to a critical decision point—would stand up with me and say "Enough!"

In my own journey, my cause felt like a complete and total failure, and my envisioned future seemed like a fleeting dream.

In the months that followed, as I walked across campus, I was afraid whenever I saw those I had once called my "brothers." I was no longer a member of any fraternal organization. I no longer knew whom I could trust, and the plan I had set for myself was in shambles.

"Follow your bliss and the universe will open doors for you where there were only walls," Joseph Campbell, author of *The Hero with a Thousand Faces*, said.

Campbell's words rang true in my own journey; where there had been only walls, doors appeared and were opened for me.

The men I had called "brothers" for two years as a member of the second fraternity were now threatening to harm me. On the other hand, I had my friends and former fraternity brothers, Chris, Joe, and Trevor—three members of the Theta Chi Fraternity I had left two-and-a-half years before—who demonstrated courage, loyalty, and offered a helping hand in one of the darkest and most terrifying moments of my life.

With these thoughts in mind, I petitioned Theta Chi's international leaders for the opportunity to return to Theta Chi. I had no leverage with them whatsoever, and the only rationale for my request was that I had experienced the power of fraternity men demonstrating the highest values of their organization. The only thing I could offer them was my promise to do everything in my power to live up to those very same values for the rest of my life.

Thankfully, the men of Theta Chi opened a door for me. A number of them from the then-closed Theta Chi chapter at my school provided letters of support to the fraternity's leadership on my behalf. The headquarters staff and international officers also maintained an open mind and granted my request, thereby opening a door for me where there had been only walls.

Everything else, from my decision to pursue a career in higher education, to studying hazing for my master's thesis, to my involvement in the hazing prevention movement, and eventually to writing this book, is a reflection of my commitment to pay forward the incredible gift they've given me.

SUMMARY

"Furthermore, we have not even to risk the adventure alone; for the heroes of all time have gone before us, the labyrinth is fully known; we have only to follow the thread of the hero-path," Campbell wrote. "And where we had thought to find an abomination, we shall find a god; where we had thought to slay another, we shall slay ourselves; where we had thought to travel outward, we shall come to the center of our own existence; where we had thought to be alone, we shall be with all the world."

The reward I gained from my journey was not only returning to the fraternity I had left three years before or the brothers-turned-friends-turned-brothers again who confronted a hostile situation to save me; it was also the treasure I found within myself. In Chapter 6, I discussed how I had never seen myself as much of a leader, but beginning with that moment on April 26, 2000, I began to believe in my own capacity and potential as a leader. I had found my "hero-path."

When we begin our hero's journey, we may focus on the change we will create in our organizations, communities, or world, but in the end, the greatest and most profound transformation is often the one within us.

PART V
CHANGING YOUR WORLD

"You cannot get through a single day without having an impact on the world around you. What you do makes a difference, and you have to decide what kind of difference you want to make."

— Jane Goodall

CHAPTER 20

DESCENDING THE MOUNTAIN

"A candle loses nothing by lighting another candle."

— James Keller

In this book, almost all of our focus has been on ourselves. From Chapters 4 and 5 where we considered our callings, gifts, and talents and the doubts and insecurities that might hold us back, to Chapters 8 to 14 where we equipped ourselves with the perspectives, skills, and training for our own hero's journey, and to Chapters 15 to 17, where we confronted our greatest threats, namely our foes, our fears, and our failures. Now that we've learned what it takes to be a hero, it's time for us to turn our attention to creating and sustaining change in our organizations, communities, and world.

Leaders ascend mountains, but heroes come back down.

One of my favorite scenes in the Marvel Cinematic Universe is when the Ancient One, as she is dying, delivers a few final insights to Doctor Strange as the "astral forms" of the two characters look out a hospital window.

"You wonder what I see in your future?" the Ancient One asks.

"No," Doctor Strange replies, before correcting his response to a "yes," as the Ancient One casts an incredulous look in his direction.

"I never saw your future, only its possibilities," the Ancient One says. "You have such a capacity for goodness. You've always excelled, but not because you crave success but because of your fear of failure."

"It's what made me a great doctor," Strange responds.

"It's precisely what's kept you from greatness," the Ancient One admonishes. "Arrogance and fear still keep you from learning the simplest and most significant lesson of all."

"Which is?"

"It's not about you," the Ancient One firmly, but gently, implores.

In our own hero's journey, it is easy to get so caught up in what we are trying to do that we forget the journey is not about us. The journey is only a vehicle for us to give our best to something larger than ourselves. In other words, if our journey does not serve and uplift anyone but us, it isn't really a hero's journey.

In the great hero stories told throughout history, the hero's tale did not end with triumph, but instead with some sort of service to the hero's people. The journey is not about the triumph, but rather the impact on others.

In the *Epic of Gilgamesh*, an epic poem dating to 2100 BCE from ancient Mesopotamia, the hero Gilgamesh experiences a fantastic journey, culminating in him obtaining a plant that has the power to restore one's youth. A snake then steals the plant, and Gilgamesh returns with empty hands, but also with a knowledge and acceptance of his own mortality. This helps the hero see that, through his legacy—that is, his contributions to his community and the experiences, learnings, and truths he shares with others—he can, in fact, achieve immortality.

What do you do to help others, whether individuals or organizations, find their own potential?

When you reach the goals you have for yourself, do you go back to your organization or your community to help others find their potential? Or do you simply say, "I've done my time"?

As Dr. Martin Luther King, Jr., maybe the greatest civil rights leader of all time, observed, "Life's most persistent and urgent question is, 'What are you doing for others?'"

By focusing our journey on others, rather than ourselves, we become more than leaders. We become heroes, even in the most improbable places.

FROM THE BEST OF TIMES

When you think about where you may find heroes, what kinds of places come to mind?

Did "corporate boardroom" make the list?

Few people think of C-suites when they are looking for heroes, and even fewer think of the corner office of an airline industry company, but that is precisely where we will find one of the best examples of a leader who kept a laser-like focus on serving and uplifting others.

In 1967, Herb Kelleher and Rollin King founded Southwest Airlines, then an intrastate carrier operating solely within the state of Texas. By 2014, it carried more US passengers than any other domestic airline. Southwest has posted profits for more than forty consecutive years in the financially fickle airline industry, which has seen thirty bankruptcies since 2000, including well-known carriers such as American Airlines, Delta Airlines, United Airlines, and US Airways (twice).

Southwest now serves more than 100 million people each year, and it consistently ranks at or near the top of every metric for customer satisfaction.

But, of course, there is more to the success of Southwest Airlines than its numbers, and that success starts at the top with co-founder and former CEO, Herb Kelleher. In fact, Southwest may have sacrificed some level of financial success in order to put first things first.

In a 2013 interview with *Fortune*, Kelleher was asked about leading through tough times, when the economy is not doing as well. "We could have made more money if we'd furloughed people during numerous events over the last forty years, but we never have. We didn't think it was the right thing to do."

It's not the right thing to do.

Many people chalk up Southwest's success to Kelleher's infectious, larger-than-life personality. He is famous for drafting the business model for Southwest on the back of a cocktail napkin, and he is known as a bourbon-drinking, chain-smoking, cowboy hat-wearing maverick.

One thing that separates Southwest Airlines from its competitors is its focus on people, specifically, its focus on its *own* people—its employees. In this company's culture, employees come first, customers second, and shareholders third. Those values lead the way for Kelleher and the company he co-founded.

"I've always thought that having a simple set of values for a company was also a very efficient and expedient way to go," Kelleher said. "And I'll tell you why. Because if somebody makes a proposal and it infringes on those values, you don't study it for two years. You just say, 'No, we don't do that.' And you go on quickly."

When asked by *Fortune* magazine about leaders from other companies who would come to Southwest to see how it achieved such consistent success, Kelleher said, "Many of them, I think, were looking for some formula, you know, that you could put on the blackboard. The concept is simple, but the execution takes a lot of work and a lot of attention. If you're going to pay personal attention to each of your people, for instance, and every grief and every joy that they suffer in their lives, you really have to have a tremendous network for gathering information. We want to show them they're important to us as who they are, as people."

By focusing on others, rather than on himself, Kelleher was able to achieve a level of success that so many other leaders can only dream of. Indeed, even in retiring as CEO of the company he co-founded, he is mindful of creating the right conditions for the next CEO to find his own success.

"I deliberately decided in deference to Gary's leadership that I should take a much lower profile. It involves, for instance, not going to a number of company events, like the chili cook-off, because I didn't want anybody to think that I was competing for attention with our new leader," Kelleher said.

It isn't about Kelleher, the co-founder, the former CEO, the leader. It's about everybody else.

Through a genuine, honest, and persistent commitment to serving and uplifting others, Kelleher was able to create a culture of success that far outpaced any of his peers. It may be cliché, but as former President Harry Truman once said, "It is amazing what you can accomplish if you do not care who gets the credit."

TO THE WORST OF TIMES

It's easier to give credit when there is a lot of credit to go around, right? After all, when a company has forty consecutive years of success, it is a lot easier to implement and maintain a culture focused on others.

What about when times are tough?

Can you imagine any time tougher than when a parent loses a child?

In February 2018, the parents of fifteen children who died from hazing came together for the first time to talk about how they could prevent other parents from going through what they had gone through, according to a February 23, 2018 story in *The State* by Bristow Marchant.

"Whether you lose your life by hazing or by gunshot, I want us all to come together," said Robert Champion, whose son by the same name died from hazing at Florida A&M University in 2011. "We're stronger together, and we can make a difference."

Although it would be easy, and completely understandable, for these parents and families to focus on their own lawsuits and legal settlements and on testifying in cases to hold accountable anyone and everyone who had a role in their child's death, these parents are choosing a more courageous path. They're choosing to use their pain to make a positive difference in others' lives.

One of the hazing victims, Dalton Debrick, had told his mother shortly before his death that he no longer intended to pursue a career in engineering, but was now planning to become a coach and teacher. "He's going to make a difference in kids' lives, but not the way he thought," his mother, Debbie Debrick, said.

For an even more dramatic example of helping and serving others even in the very worst of times, consider the story of one man who was on a three-month business trip on one of the most fateful days in the world's history.

On August 6, a twenty-nine-year-old businessman was planning to return home from his three-month-long trip 400-some miles away from home. His wife and infant son were eagerly awaiting his return.

Around 8:15 that morning, the businessman observed a plane flying overhead and saw it drop a small object with a parachute. Suddenly, the entire sky was aflame, and the businessman was hurled into a nearby potato patch.

It was 1945, and the businessman, Tsutomu Yamaguchi, was standing only two miles from where the atomic bomb was dropped on Hiroshima.

Alive, but severely injured, Yamaguchi made his way home to be with his wife and son. Finally, on August 8, Yamaguchi reached home. His condition was so severe that his own mother accused him of being a ghost and friends he had known for years did not even recognize him.

Incredibly, Yamaguchi got out of bed the following day and somehow made his way to work. Because he was an engineer, there was a lot of interest in his account of how one bomb could level an entire city.

At 11:00 a.m. on August 9, he found himself in a meeting with a company director. The director demanded a detailed report of what Yamaguchi had seen in Hiroshima. The director could not believe what he was hearing and even accused Yamaguchi of being mad.

During that same meeting, Yamaguchi again saw a blinding white flash and immediately dove to the ground. This time, an atomic bomb had been dropped on Nagasaki, the city where Yamaguchi lived and worked.

Fortunately, through an incredible twist of fate, Yamaguchi's wife and son survived, despite their house being completely destroyed. Because of Yamaguchi's severe wounds, his wife and son had left the house to obtain ointment for him and were able to find shelter in a tunnel when the bomb was dropped. In other words, if Yamaguchi had not been in Hiroshima when the first atomic bomb was dropped, it is likely all three members of his family would have been at home when the second bomb was dropped, and all three would have perished.

No matter how Yamaguchi may have chosen to react to his situation, no one could fault him in any way for whatever he may have done, right? If he and his family were to hide in the biggest, deepest, most secure bunker ever, you could see where that would make a lot of sense.

So what did Yamaguchi do?

After avoiding discussing his experiences until the 2000s, he became one of the most outspoken proponents of nuclear disarmament, even speaking in front of the United Nations in 2006.

"Having experienced atomic bombings twice and survived, it is my destiny to talk about it," Yamaguchi said.

In whatever situation we find ourselves, whether record-breaking success or unimaginable tragedy, we have the opportunity to look beyond ourselves for chances to serve and uplift those around us. When we do that, we do more than lead—we leave a legacy.

THE LEVELS OF LEGACY

In September 2011, in Miami, Florida, best-selling author Brad Meltzer gave a TEDx talk titled, "How to Write Your Own Obituary." As morbid as that topic may sound, Meltzer's talk is really about the legacy you leave others throughout your life.

While weaving in a number of examples from his own life, Meltzer describes that leaving a legacy is as simple as first considering who will be influenced by your life and then determining what kind of influence you will have.

There are four types of legacy you can leave:

1. **Personal Legacy:** This legacy concerns anyone you affect directly through one-to-one interactions; for example, a teacher who was one of the first people to identify and recognize your potential.

2. **Family Legacy:** This legacy is how you help or support the people closest to you. It may even include your closest circle of friends, who are the family you choose, as opposed to the family you are born into.

3. **Community Legacy:** This legacy affects the place you live or the organizations or communities you belong to. In discussing community legacy, Meltzer shares a beautiful example of Jumbo's restaurant in Liberty City, Florida. Shortly after taking over the restaurant's operations in 1967, owner Bobby Flam decided to hire three black employees at a time when many restaurants had all white staffs. In fact, Flam said in a 2014 *New York Times* article that most of his thirty to thirty-five white staff members quit within a month.

    This bold stand separated Jumbo's from every other restaurant in the area. It was no longer just another restaurant; it was a part of the community and a symbol. In fact, Jumbo's was completely undamaged when rioting erupted in Liberty City in 1980, following the acquittal of four white police officers who had been charged in the beating death of a black man. The nearby area sustained more than $100 million in property damage.

".Jumbo's was among the first restaurants to have blacks not just washing dishes, but running the cash register and serving the food—it was not to be defiled," said Dr. Marvin Dunn, author of *Black Miami in the Twentieth Century.* "That's where people went after they finished rioting."

4. **Complete Strangers Legacy:** This legacy affects people you have never and will never meet. It is the ripple effect of the causes and issues you stand for, spreading out to countless people beyond the reach of your own direct work. It is the torch passed from you to the people you reach through your personal, family, and community legacies, and those people then push your legacy to innumerable others.

Your legacy is how you, no matter who you are or where you live, can change the world.

EXERCISE

What are your personal, family, community, and complete stranger legacies? For each of the four categories, identify who is within that category in your own life, as well as one Specific, Measurable, Action-Oriented, Reasonable, and Time-Bound (SMART) goal for that part of your legacy.

Who is affected by your Personal Legacy? What is one SMART goal that will help you create the Personal Legacy you want?

_____

_____

_____

Who is affected by your Family Legacy? What is one SMART goal that will help you create the Family Legacy you want?

_____

_____

_____

Who is affected by your Community Legacy? What is one SMART goal that will help you create the Community Legacy you want?

_____

_____

_____

Who is affected by your Complete Strangers Legacy? What is one SMART goal that will help you create the Legacy with Complete Strangers that you want?

_____

_____

_____

SUMMARY

A leader goes up the mountain, but a hero returns from the top. Heroes do not just achieve results; they also empower, equip, and train others to produce those results.

Much of what we do is the result of our ambitions for ourselves. Achievement, fulfillment, and success are things we chase for the effect they will have on our own lives, not the lives of others.

In the course of our self-pursuits, however, we sometimes stumble on the opportunity to make a difference for others and to leave a legacy. As we travel through our journeys, we fight, we fall, and we rise. Despite everything we put into our journeys, one simple truth remains: Your legacy is not for you. Your legacy is the gift you give to others through your journey.

We find that the things we do for ourselves pass away with us, but the things we do for others last forever. Once we see this difference and feel the effect we can have on others, our lives and missions are transformed.

When we focus on pursuing our own interests, it is easy to lose sight of opportunities to serve and uplift others. By inviting others into our journeys, we not only leave behind an uplifting legacy, but we empower others to live that legacy, too.

CHAPTER 21

PAVING THE WAY

"Good actions give strength to ourselves and
inspire good actions in others."

— Plato

As a child of the 1980s, one of my proudest moments was introducing
my own children to the video games I loved playing when I was young.
I may have been just a little impatient in that process, purchasing the
original *Super Mario Bros.* for my sons when my oldest was just five
years old and my youngest was still working on the whole walking thing.

However, despite my impatience, and the subsequent amount of time
I've spent playing the classic video game with my children, it has provided a valuable leadership lesson.

LEADERSHIP IN SIGHT

As someone who first played *Super Mario Bros.* on the original Nin-
tendo console, it is easy to fall into old patterns of racing through each
level, even with a newer, somewhat unfamiliar gaming console.

However, when playing with multiple players, it is important to remain "in frame," lest one's lagging partners are dropped into pits or pushed into enemies along the way. Of course, to remain in sight requires heroes to expose themselves a little longer to the dangers before them, whether they be fire chomps, koopa troopa, or any of the many other threats.

The lesson here is that, in our own hero's journey, we must remain "in sight" for others, paving the way for their success. If we don't remain in sight, it's probable that our partners will fall, and our efforts to lead others to the next level will fail. That is, it is important to lead our groups, organizations, and communities from within their frames, meeting them wherever they are in their own journeys, in order to lead them through the challenge. We can't race ahead out of sight, leaving them to navigate the path and the threats on their own.

This lesson is not only relevant to the world of one heroic plumber and his brother, but also to one of the greatest movements of all time—the Civil Rights Movement.

In the early twentieth century, Booker T. Washington and W. E. B. Du Bois were the two most influential African-American men in the United States. Although they differed in their perspectives and preferred strategies, together they paved the way for many of the civil rights gains made in the 1950s and 1960s. Du Bois, in particular, had a direct connection to the most recognizable leaders of the movement through Septima Poinsette Clark, who became known as the "Grandmother" of the Civil Rights Movement.

After beginning her life as a highly respected faculty member at Booker T. Washington High School in Columbia, South Carolina, Clark began studying at Columbia University in New York City and with W. E. B. Du Bois at Atlanta University in Georgia.

Du Bois, who believed education and civil rights were the only path to equality, had a clear influence on Clark, who once said, "Knowledge could empower marginalized groups in ways that formal legal equality couldn't."

Clark leveraged her belief in the power of education and civil rights and her background as a gifted teacher to lead workshops for young activists.

In 1955, Rosa Parks participated in one of Clark's workshops shortly before her arrest for not yielding her seat later that year. "At that time, I was very nervous, very troubled in my mind about the events that were occurring in Montgomery," Parks said later. "But then I had the chance to work with Septima. She was such a calm and dedicated person in the midst of all that danger. I thought, 'If I could only catch some of her spirit.' I wanted to have the courage to accomplish the kinds of things that she had been doing for years."

We may have the knowledge and power to find some levels of success on our own, but when we guide others through each step of their own journeys, together we can reach even higher levels of success.

An oft-cited proverb states, "If you want to go quickly, go alone. If you want to go far, go together."

In the causes we care about, the distance we desire to travel is far greater than any one person can go. By bringing others into the cause, by paving the way for them, and by uniting our collective causes into a larger vision, we find the path to change not only our groups and communities but the whole world.

THE POWER OF COMMON PURPOSE

When speaking of traveling great distances and changing the world, it is impossible not to reference the legacy of Amelia Earhart.

As a result of her pioneering feats as the first woman to fly across the Atlantic Ocean (1928), the first woman to fly across the North American continent (1928), the first woman to fly solo nonstop across the Atlantic Ocean (1932), and the first pilot of any gender to fly solo from Honolulu, Hawaii, to Oakland, California (1935), Earhart became one of the brightest stars of her time.

Earhart, who had experienced her own obstacles and opposition in a male-dominated career, sought to use her celebrity status to help other women pursue careers that had been previously closed to them. She became a member of the National Women's Party and advocated for the Equal Rights Amendment.

In 1934, when Edward C. Elliott, President of Purdue University, heard Amelia Earhart speak at an event in New York City, he asked her to come to Purdue to speak to the women students there about their post-college opportunities. Soon thereafter, Elliott was able to convince Earhart to come to Purdue on a longer-term basis.

Earhart became a visiting faculty member at Purdue beginning in 1935, where she also served as an advisor to aeronautical engineering and as a career counselor to women students at the school. While she was there, she lived in South Hall and became the most sought-after lunch table companion for the female students living there.

Although Earhart disappeared during her attempt to circumnavigate the globe in 1937, she not only led the way by her example, but she invested her time, energy, and insights into helping others push against the boundaries and limitations they faced in a male-dominated world.

Earhart's example broke barriers, but her investment in others changed the world. When people come together around a common purpose and ideal, they not only possess the goal of changing the world but the means to do so, as well.

EXERCISE

Name two or three people, or a group of people, you could invite to share a larger legacy with you. In what ways could you empower them to enlarge that legacy and make it their own?

_____

_____

_____

What concerns do you have about inviting others into a larger legacy?

_____

_____

_____

What are some ways you could calm some of those concerns?

_____

_____

_____

THE POWER OF ORGANIZATIONS

Have you ever thought about why the founders of many fraternal organizations chose Greek letters and mottoes for their organizations? In addition to my own membership in a "Greek" organization, I spent the first nine years of my career working with fraternities and sororities, and I've always been fascinated by the beginnings of those organizations.

More than a simple case of cultural appropriation, the founders of fraternal organizations were endeavoring to create Hellenistic societies, organizations committed to developing the Hellenistic ideals of rational thinking and reasoning, the pursuit of knowledge and the arts, moderation, civic responsibility, and physical development. This idea is at the core of almost every fraternity and sorority.

Through these Hellenistic societies, the creators of these organizations sought to transform their members, and through their members, the world around them. By connecting their members, their activities, and their operations to Hellenistic ideals, and by teaching their members to act on moral principles and values, the founders were creating the kinds of men and women who could change the world in positive and profound ways.

It is no coincidence that so many of the early leaders of our nation also were members of these societies. By acting on those values, the founders understood they were empowering their members to be leaders in their communities and within the larger society. In this way, they were fostering transformational leadership.

With these noble goals, they looked to classical philosophers, such as Aristotle, Heraclitus, Plato, and Socrates, to show the way.

As quoted before, "Whatever we learn to do, we learn by actually doing it: men come to be builders, for instance, by building, and harp players by playing the harp," Aristotle said. "In the same way, by doing just acts, we come to be just; by doing self-controlled acts, we come to be self-controlled; and by doing brave acts, we become brave."

Aristotle's idea is far from just a product of some ancient way of thinking or a primitive understanding of human development. Modern neurological research has discovered that the brain organizes behavior patterns in the very same way Aristotle articulated 2,300 years ago.

From a physiological perspective, the more you engage in a particular behavior, the more the brain cells involved in that behavior will grow and form newer, stronger connections among the cells that are part of that behavior. When the pathway among those cells is complete, it takes less concentration for you to perform that task. The behavior that used to require concentration and focus becomes an automatic, natural response.

Modern science, it appears, has caught up to classical philosophy. We create who we are by the things we do.

Taking that idea one step farther, the organizations we participate in not only describe or reflect the people we are; they actually create who we are. They create our behaviors and identities through activities and operations, through those things that are discussed—or not discussed—at meetings, and through informal interactions. They create who we are by what we do and by what we don't do.

With this discovery in mind, if we want to create groups of people who band together to create positive change in the world, our organizations must create patterns of behavior that foster the Heroic Arts we discussed in Chapters 8 through 14, while also limiting the types of behaviors that undermine those goals.

In Chapter 3, we discussed how the purpose of the initiation or onboarding process must be clear, productive, and self-evident. In the absence of those characteristics, the initiate is left feeling that the experience itself is the purpose. Considering the added layer of changes in the brain's physical structure when destructive patterns like hazing are introduced and reinforced, it is easy to see how even a small deviation from a positive and productive rite of passage can create a culture that embraces hazing above any other organizational purpose.

In this way, even one seemingly small deviation can have disastrous effects on the organization's health, much like the characteristics of a fractal—a never-ending pattern, created by repeating a relatively simple process over and over. Fractals make beautiful, mesmerizing images. Clouds, coastlines, hurricanes, mountains, and seashells are just some of the examples of fractals you can find in nature.

Much like Aristotle and brain development, fractals illustrate that the smallest behaviors, repeated consistently over time, can create the largest transformations.

This idea can be applied to individual members or small groups as representatives of the larger organization. If one member or group is acting in a way that counters or frustrates the purpose and values of the larger organization, anyone who comes into contact with that person or interacts with that group will think that member or small group represents the true nature of the larger organization.

To the outside observer, the organization is what they see from the individual or small group. Then, the larger the audience that outside observer has, the more he or she is able to influence others and how they see that larger organization.

For a light-hearted example, consider my wife's experience with my fraternity brothers. As she met me and my closest fraternity brothers from my school, she became convinced that we were the "nerd" fraternity, that is, an organizational home for nerds across the United States. It was not until she met my brothers from other schools that her perception of our organization changed.

How do you see this phenomenon play out in your own organization? Are there groups or organizations you see in one way that are something else entirely? In fact, we make these kinds of judgments every day.

One saying you may have heard throughout your life is that you can't control what others think of you. Although that may be accurate to some degree, I think that saying is an abdication of one's personal responsibility. In truth, as an individual or organization, you can significantly influence what others think of you by the things you do.

When you act with congruence, aligning the small pieces of your organization, your group, or your life with the bigger picture you desire, you are making possible a powerful transformation in your community, your organization, your own life, and the lives of others. By getting the little things right, we get the bigger picture right, too.

But in doing so, we cannot forget the importance of engaging others in the larger solution. On our own, even our best, most noble intentions can create only short-term solutions, or worse yet, can make those we're trying to help dependent on us. Together, however, we have the opportunity to create solutions that build up and empower others, thereby having a lasting, long-term influence on our communities and the larger society.

EXERCISE

By getting the little things right, we get the bigger things right.

If you are involved in a group or organization, how do your activities, meetings, and operations reflect your group's priorities? How do they distract from your group's priorities? Or maybe you have one person who distracts from your group's priorities. How does that person misrepresent the mission of your organization?

_____

_____

_____

What is one small change you could make in your group's activities, meetings, or operations that would more closely align the things your group does with the group's priorities? If one person is distracting others from the group's priorities, how might you address the effect of that person's actions with them?

_____

_____

_____

THE POWER OF PAVING THE WAY

"Here I come to save the day!" The words and music of the _Mighty Mouse_ theme are familiar and triumphant, and the diminutive hero has been beloved for generations. But does the pint-sized punch-thrower also point to our greatest weakness as human beings? Or worse yet, does the "Mighty Mouse" syndrome hold us back?

It is great to be a hero. There is the glory of swooping in at the most critical moment and the satisfaction of having made a real difference in the lives of others, not to mention being given keys to various cities, talk show appearances, and ticker tape parades. (Results may vary.) But do you want to save the day, or do you want to save the world?

To save the day, you need only swoop in and swoop out. The focus is on the immediate remedy, not the long-term solution, which makes it a good bet that you'll be back soon.

An old parable of a young boy on a beach demonstrates not only our desire to save the day, but also how little steps can lead us to the bigger goal we're pursuing.

One day, an old man was walking along a beach covered with thousands of starfish that had been brought ashore with the tide. As the man walked down the shore, he came upon a young boy who was picking up the starfish and gleefully throwing them back into the ocean, one by one.

Puzzled, the man looked at the boy and asked what he was doing. Without looking up from his task, the boy simply replied, "I'm saving these starfish, sir."

The old man laughed out loud, "There are thousands of starfish and only one of you. What difference can you make?"

The boy picked up a starfish, tossed it into the water, turned to the man, and said, "I made a difference to that one!"

To that one, he made a difference.

But why stop there? What happens if the young boy isn't there the next time the starfish wash up on the beach? If our ultimate goal is to make a difference in our communities and our organizations, we cannot just save that one, and the next one, and the one after that. It is important not only to "save the day," but also to "pave the way."

Looking at the greatest heroes chronicled throughout this book, we can see example after example of ordinary people who not only broke through their own barriers, but also engaged, served, and uplifted others. In this way, those heroes not only made a difference; they transformed the world.

SUMMARY

All of us are blessed with amazing experiences. From those moments that bring us to our knees to those when we feel like we are on top of the world, each and every one of us has our own experiences and lessons. Through those lessons, we find great strengths and truths, and these treasures give us the tools we need to transform ourselves, our organizations, our communities, and even our world.

But these tools are not ours to keep; they are ours to teach.

Joseph Campbell said, "When we quit thinking primarily about ourselves and our own self-preservation, we undergo a truly heroic transformation of consciousness."

Through your hero's journey, you have changed, you have grown, and you have become more and more the person you have the power to be. As a result, you are not only committing to living and owning that new identity, but also becoming a mentor for others as they embark on their own hero's journey.

By building up others, we build our organizations, our communities, and even our world.

CHAPTER 22

MAKING CHANGE STICK

"It is time to stop waiting for someone to save us. It is time to face the truth of our situation—that we're all in this together, that we all have a voice—and figure out how to mobilize the hearts and minds of everyone in our workplaces and communities."

— Margaret Wheatley

At the end of the hero's journey, we find accomplishment and contentment awaiting us. Rest assured that we have created positive change or made a difference in our groups, our communities, or even our world. Every feline has been rescued from every tree, every busy street traversed by both young and old, and every super villain referred to the nearest asylum, hospital, or prison.

But there is no retirement home for heroes. Heroes continue moving forward to lead change within their organizations, communities, or worlds, while also concluding one journey and launching the next.

CHANGE IS THE ONLY CONSTANT

After an arduous and perilous journey, fairy tales, legends, and modern cinema tell us that the hero rides into the town square and delivers the elixir, an item that solves the very problem the town was desperately trying to solve. The townspeople spill out into the streets and unite in celebration as the hero quietly slips away and rides off into the sunset.

But this isn't how the real world works. If you attempted the same stunt in your organization or your community, you probably could find your magic solution precisely where you left it. You would find it unconsidered, unnoticed, and altogether untouched. If not, you may find it moved to the nearest trash receptacle.

Countless blogs, books, and seminars have been devoted to the challenge of leading change, but the biggest takeaway is that making change stick is not just a destination or an outcome but an ongoing process. It is a process of changing, healing, and above all, leading.

Heraclitus, one of the great ancient Greek philosophers, once said, "No man ever steps in the same river twice, for it's not the same river and he's not the same man."

This is a reminder that change is the only constant; therefore, the only way we will succeed is through a constant approach to change.

Dr. Martin Luther King, Jr., once remarked, "Change does not roll in on the wheels of inevitability but comes through continuous struggle."

Ongoing struggle is not what most of us signed up for. In our world, particularly in Western society, we value accomplishment, achievement, and the completion of tasks. Entire industries have sprung up around planners, software applications, and organizational strategies to get more and more done.

We glorify "done," but many of the changes we desire to make in our groups, communities, and world are not as simple and easily marked done as a chore at home, an event in our organization, or a project at work.

Change is not accomplished once; change is accomplished every day.

CAUTION: FALLING ROCK

In Greek mythology, Sisyphus was the king of Ephyra. He was best known for his hubris and trickery, thinking he was even cleverer than the Greek gods. As a punishment, Sisyphus was made to roll an enormous boulder up a huge hill for all eternity. This punishment was made even more maddening by the Greek god Zeus, who had enchanted the boulder to roll away just before reaching the top of the hill. As a result, Sisyphus was condemned to an eternity of futile efforts and never-ending frustration.

When the changes we make are not anchored in the group or society's culture, we risk a Sisyphean fate, fighting the same fights over and over again until the end of time. In the context of the fight against hazing, we may implement some changes in an organization that ends hazing for one or two years, but anyone who has worked with college students knows that the smallest slip can send this enormous boulder rolling back down the hill.

For this reason, the hero's journey does not have an end; rather, it is a commitment to continuous struggle. In the words of Joseph Campbell, "The hero is the champion of things becoming, not of things become."

John Kotter, Konosuke Matsushita Professor of Leadership, Emeritus, at the Harvard Business School and prolific author on the topics of business, change, and leadership, wrote the seminal work in the field of change management, *Leading Change.*

In that book, Kotter outlines the eight steps for change management:

1. Establishing a Sense of Urgency
2. Creating the Guiding Coalition
3. Developing a Vision and Strategy
4. Communicating the Change Vision
5. Empowering Employees for Broad-Based Action
6. Generating Short-Term Wins
7. Consolidating Gains and Producing More Change
8. Anchoring New Approaches in the Culture

It's no coincidence that many of these steps also can be seen through the lens of the hero's journey, which could be described as history's first change management framework. After all, Campbell discovered the common themes of the hero's journey after studying mythology and storytelling throughout the world. The hero stories our ancestors told for countless generations were not just thrilling adventures but blueprints for growth and personal development.

In Kotter's model, the last two steps are identified as those where "implementing and sustaining the change" occur. In the seventh step, "Consolidating Gains and Producing More Change," leaders continue to direct energy into the process through new projects, themes, and change agents, thereby protecting against indifference and stagnation.

Finally, in "Anchoring New Approaches in the Culture," leaders attend to the processes that secure and support the changes in the culture and fabric of the organization, including everything from onboarding new members to transitioning leaders.

In the next two sections, we will focus on these two components for implementing and sustaining change: funneling energy into the change process and supporting people through the process.

THE LAWS OF ENERGY

When we talk about the dynamics among individuals, particularly in a group setting, we refer to them as "energy." Why do we use that word? Among individuals, you can feel something that is palpable and powerful, yet not visible. It seems to exist in the space among people. In addition, this type of energy manifests many of the same properties as the type of energy we learn about in physics and science classes.

The three laws of energy, listed below, are not only relevant in the realms of physical sciences, but also in the energy necessary to propel change in our organizations and communities.

1. An object in motion will stay in motion.

The first law of motion states that an object in motion will stay in motion, unless acted on by another force. In this case, that force may be apathy, fear, or frustration. Whatever the force may be, it is up to you to continue directing energy into the change process, as Kotter described in the seventh step, "Consolidating Gains and Producing More Change."

2. For every action there is an equal and opposite reaction.

You did not arrive at the final stage of the hero's journey by having someone preach to you; you gained this experience by digging deep within yourself and finding the strength you already had within.

As you discovered in Chapter 6, nobody did the digging for you. A mentor, or maybe even the examples in this book, helped you find the "gold vein" in your own life, but you were the one who did the real work of uncovering it.

Likewise, no one else will gain this experience through your preaching. The more you push, the more others will push back. Share your experience one piece at a time, one person at a time, and allow the other person to discover the gold.

3. Energy can be neither created nor destroyed; it can only be transformed.

Gather together with like-minded people and imagine the possibilities. As Kotter writes in his sixth step, small wins maintain momentum. However, big dreams embolden and excite us. The greater the challenge, the greater the motivation to succeed. Are you more likely to motivate people to do what everybody else is doing or to be revolutionary? Do you tweak or transform?

Share your vision with others, and leave space for them not only to see themselves in that vision, but to make it bigger and bolder.

THE MINDS OF MEN AND WOMEN

Whenever we, as humans, are faced with change, it is natural for us to feel threatened. In fact, modern neuroscience has shown that our brains respond to social threats in the very same ways they respond to physical threats. When that threat response, which you may know as "fight or flight," is engaged, the primitive, reactionary parts of our brains take control, pushing our more sophisticated, rationale thoughts aside. But being aware of this natural response also gives us insights for guiding others through change.

Dr. David Rock, who coined the term "Neuroleadership" and serves as the Director of the NeuroLeadership Institute, introduced the SCARF model for helping individuals navigate change.

The SCARF model consists of five domains of motivation that can activate either the reward or threat mechanisms in people's brains:

1. **Status** is about relative importance to others. Example: "I am valuable."
2. **Certainty** concerns being able to predict the future. Example: "I know where I stand."
3. **Autonomy** provides a sense of control over events. Example: "I have a choice."
4. **Relatedness** is a sense of safety with others—of friend rather than foe. Example: "I belong."
5. **Fairness** is a perception of fair exchanges between people. Example: "I am treated fairly."

When we recognize these as positive or negative motivations, either potential rewards or threats, we can choose strategies for motivating others in positive ways, rather than activating negative responses that may result from the absence of one or more of these domains.

For example, a lack of clear expectations or outcomes may result in a negative response based on the certainty domain, whereas a lack of clear and consistent ground rules may trigger a threat response based on the fairness domain. By breaking a project into smaller steps and leading by example in the process, you can create positive reward responses for these domains.

THE NEXT JOURNEY

At the moment you think you have achieved everything you can achieve, you either choose to stop living or to start venturing. For those who have chosen the hero's journey, there is no cruise control, no pause button, and no vacation.

The hero's journey is always depicted as a circle, rather than a straight line. It is a journey, not a destination.

"Standing still is the fastest way of moving backwards in a rapidly changing world," said classic Hollywood star Lauren Bacall.

As a teenager in the 1990s, for me one of the greatest examples of overcoming the temptation to stand still was the Chicago Bulls. The team won six championships in eight seasons, a feat that probably will not be seen again in any of the four major US sports.

One of the most oft-cited clichés of the sports world is that it is much more difficult to win a second consecutive championship than to win the first. The reason is if you put forth the exact same level of performance the second time, chances are everyone else already is prepared to match, or to surpass, that level of performance.

Imagine the focus, motivation, and strength it must have taken for one team to win six championships in eight years. In 1992-93, for example, the Bulls won fifty-seven games, which meant they ceded home-court advantage to their Eastern Conference Finals and NBA Finals opponents, the New York Knicks and Phoenix Suns, who won sixty and sixty-two games that year, respectively. Those Knicks and Suns teams were loaded with some of the most decorated and prolific players of the season, as well as the Coach of the Year (the Knicks' Pat Riley) and Most Valuable Player (the Suns' Charles Barkley).

The following season, Michael Jordan abruptly retired following his father's murder, saying he had lost his passion for the game. Despite the departure and tragedy faced by the team's star player, that year the Bulls still managed to win fifty-five games, only two fewer than the year before.

The 1993-94 season, more than the three championship years before it, demonstrated the team's commitment to moving forward, despite losing, arguably, the greatest player in NBA history.

Throughout the six championships won by the team, it was easy to see the level of commitment demonstrated by every individual, from the star players to the last players on the bench, and from the coaches on the sideline to the staff in the front office. After all, the trophies at the ends of those seasons served as proof. However, we cannot overlook the commitment also present during the seasons of adversity and struggle.

When you believe that strongly in your cause or community, you will always find ways to move forward.

EXERCISE

What are the causes, issues, or organizations that matter to you?

_____

_____

_____

Who are the people who most inspire you to step up, take a stand, and make a difference in your organization, community, or even the world?

_____

_____

_____

As you consider that cause, issue, or organization, is your commitment a single journey or a series of journeys? In either case, when and where will you begin your first journey?

_____

_____

_____

How will you answer your call to adventure? Do you want to be average and ordinary, or are you ready to be extraordinary?

_____

_____

_____

SUMMARY

At the end of this chapter, we discussed the focus, motivation, and strength of one of the greatest sports teams in the world, reflecting on the deep commitment required for that level of success. By committing ourselves to our own journeys, we are committing to progress, not perfection.

Now imagine the commitment, focus, motivation, and strength for those people who have given their whole lives to a cause, issue, or organization. You have read some of their stories throughout this book, and countless, lesser-known heroes have toiled for years on behalf of the causes they care deeply about.

From one journey to the next, they have chosen to answer the call to adventure time after time with a hearty and eager "yes."

Will you?

A FINAL NOTE

BECOMING THE HERO INSIDE OF YOU

"In order to succeed, people need a sense of self-efficacy,
to struggle together with resilience to meet the inevitable
obstacles and inequities of life."

— Albert Bandura

At the beginning of this book, you had the opportunity to choose either what is familiar and safe or what is meaningful and significant. At the end of the last chapter, you were asked a simple, two-word question: "Will you?" In the hero's journey, you have come full circle.

Now what? This book is nothing but a collection of interesting stories and inspirational fluff if you do not act on it. More than that, if you do not implement the strategies and tools presented throughout it, your life will never be any different than it is right now. So what actions are you going to take?

English author and philosopher Sir Francis Bacon wrote in *Meditationes Sacrae*, "ipsa scientia potestas est," which can be translated as, "knowledge itself is power." With all due respect to Sir Francis, knowledge itself is not power; it's the application of knowledge that is true power.

How are you going to apply your knowledge?

In the next ninety days, I challenge you to commit to at least ten Specific, Measurable, Action-Oriented, Reasonable, and Time-Bound (SMART) actions based on what you learned in this book. You may have already written one, two, or all ten of those actions in the reflective exercises throughout this book. Great! Collect the best, most exciting ones here for easy reference. Or maybe they're wholly different from what you wrote before. That's great, too! Whatever they are, they should be actions that move forward your own hero's journey.

1. _____

2. _____

3. _____

4. _____

5. _____

6. _____

7. _____

8. _____

9. _____

10. _____

If you choose to embark on the hero's journey, I am here for you. I want to be your coach and mentor through this journey, and I promise to guide you along the path and be with you every step along the way.

Now that you've finished the book and launched your journey, I invite you to contact me. I would love for you to share with me what resonated most for you and to tell me about *your* journey, even your foes, your fears, and your failures. Most of all, I would love to hear how I can help you.

I would be thrilled to offer you a complimentary, no-obligation coaching consultation by phone, by Skype, or in person, if geographically possible. The best way to reach me is by texting me with your name and your time zone on my private cell phone number, (651) 233-3533.

I wish you the very best in your journey and in helping others live their own journeys.

There is a hero in all of us.

Your friend,

ABOUT THE AUTHOR

CHAD ELLSWORTH is an author; professional keynote speaker; career, leadership, and life coach; and entrepreneur. Beginning with his earliest experiences as a college freshman and fraternity man, he has been in search of a better way to empower others to be themselves and become the best versions of themselves.

As a college junior, Chad challenged his fraternity chapter's culture of hazing, after which he was forced to move out in the middle of the night. Chad left the experience consumed by the idea that there is a better way: to bring members into organizations; to create and deliver challenging, meaningful, and positive experiences; and to provide them with the confidence, knowledge, and skills to be authentic, empowered, and values-driven in their personal and professional lives.

In graduate school, Chad conducted and published an original research study on perceptions of hazing, receiving national recognition for his work, which led him to serve as President of the Board of Directors for the non-profit organization HazingPrevention.Org. As a result of that role, he was asked to create and deliver two presentations at the Theta Chi Fraternity's 2010 National Convention and School of Fraternity Practices. The second presentation, "Building Heroes," changed his life and led to the creation of Caped Coaching, LLC.

As a professional, Chad spent seven-plus years as the Program Director for the Office for Fraternity & Sorority Life at the University of Minnesota, where he advised and mentored student leaders, developed educational and leadership development programs, and served as a liaison for the fraternity and sorority community with the campus and Minneapolis-St. Paul communities. In 2007, Chad was named an Anti-Hazing Hero by HazingPrevention.Org, and in 2010, he received one of two awards that year for Outstanding Greek Life Professionals by the Fraternity Information & Programming Group (FIPG).

Chad is a Career Coach in the Undergraduate Business Career Center at the Carlson School of Management at the University of Minnesota, where he was recognized in 2018 as Staff of the Year by a vote of the school's students. He is passionate about helping others connect their interests, passions, skills, and strengths to their personal and professional goals so they can have the opportunity to do what they do best every day.

He has been: a member of the University of Minnesota community since 2004; an Academic Advisor and interim Pre-Health Career Coach for the College of Biological Sciences; an Academic and Career Coach for the Center for Academic Planning & Exploration; Adjunct Faculty for the College of Biological Sciences, Leadership Minor, and Office of Undergraduate Education; Program Director for the Office for Fraternity & Sorority Life; and Student Activities Advisor.

Originally from Lincoln, Nebraska, Chad received his bachelor's degree from the University of Nebraska in 2001, and his master's degree from the University of Maryland in 2004. He lives in the Minneapolis-St. Paul area with his wife, Kristin, and two sons, Joey and Paul.

ABOUT CHAD ELLSWORTH CAREER, LEADERSHIP, AND LIFE COACHING

Do you look at your organization, your community, or even your own life and think, "I could be doing more to make things better?"

There is a hero in all of us. Chad Ellsworth will help you discover your passion, purpose, and power, and he will provide you with the confidence and tools to challenge the status quo, confront your fears, and change your world.

Many of us feel lost and confused because of the obligations and pressures of family, school, work, and our busy, everyday lives. We want to do something important, but we are held back by our self-limiting beliefs and destructive habits.

You don't have to resign yourself to a life that is any less than the one you dream of and hope for. Chad Ellsworth will challenge you and help you develop the confidence, strategies, and tools you need to live up to your fullest potential. He will help you make the world a better place.

Chad Ellsworth is a Board-Certified Coach and a Gallup-Certified Strengths Coach who possesses certifications for the Myers-Briggs Type Indicator and Strong Interest Inventory. He received a master's degree in Counseling and Personnel Services in 2004 and has coached hundreds of people, helping them find fulfilling careers and lives.

For more information, visit Chad's website and then text him with your name, time zone, and the best time to redeem a thirty- to sixty-minute, no-obligation coaching session by phone or Skype.

www.CapedCoaching.com
Chad@CapedCoaching.com
Mobile: 651-233-3533

BOOK CHAD ELLSWORTH TO SPEAK AT YOUR NEXT EVENT

When it comes to choosing a professional speaker for your next event, you will find no one more respected or successful—no one who will leave your audience or colleagues with more confidence or strategies for creating change—than Chad Ellsworth.

Whether your audience is ten or 10,000, in North America or abroad, Chad can deliver a customized message of inspiration for your meeting or conference. Chad understands your audience does not want to be "taught" anything, but is rather interested in hearing stories of inspiration, achievement, and real-life people challenging their status quo, confronting their fears, and changing their world.

As a result, Chad's speaking philosophy is to entertain and inspire your audience with passion and stories proven to help people transform their ordinary lives into extraordinary ones. If you are looking for a memorable speaker who will leave your audience members motivated to take on the challenges facing their organizations, communities, or own lives, book Chad Ellsworth today!

For additional information and to inquire about Chad's availability, visit his website. Then contact him by phone or email to schedule a complimentary, pre-speaking event phone interview.

www.CapedCoaching.com
Chad@CapedCoaching.com
Mobile: 651-233-3533